THERE ARE NØ DO-OVERS:

The **Big Red** Factors for Sustaining a Business Long Term

THERE ARE NØ DO-OVERS:

The **Big Red** Factors for Sustaining a Business Long Term

by Thomas Raffio with Barbara McLaughlin
and Dave Cowens

Published by Curran Pendleton Press, Raleigh, NC

Hardcover:
ISBN-10: 0988722313
ISBN-13: 978-0-9887223-1-6

Paperback:
ISBN-10: 0988722321
ISBN-13: 978-0-9887223-2-3

eBook:
ISBN-10: 098872233X
ISBN-13: 978-0-9887223-3-0

Contents

Dedications

To all my colleagues at Northeast Delta Dental and Delta Dental of Massachusetts, past and present, who've worked tirelessly through the years. And to my family — to my wife Lisa for her support and unwavering love and to our children, Jenna, Matthew, Brian, and Gabbie. Thank you for inspiring me.

— Tom Raffio

To my wife Deby. I wish I could have a do-over and be able to spend a second thirty-five years with her because she has what all enduring success is based on: integrity. Plus, she is damn good looking.

— Dave Cowens

To my dad, who long ago taught his daughter that she could do and be whatever she aspired to with no limits, and to my husband, Jim, who made all my dreams come true; he promised me the moon but gave me the whole universe. "In the morning's first kiss of sunlight, I awaken to thoughts of you. Throughout the day, you lie gently on my mind. And in the peaceful silhouettes of night, my last thoughts are still of you." (Author unknown)

— Barbara McLaughlin

Tip-off: A Word from Lew Feldstein

It is hard to imagine a dental insurance executive as a hero. I challenge you to recall the last time you saw a Pierre Cardin line of dental clothing or heard J. Lo croon about the actuary that got away. I'm willing to bet that none of you can name a dentist in public life. Yet, under Tom's leadership, Northeast Delta Dental has accomplished amazing things.

Tom Raffio, President and CEO of Northeast Delta Dental (NEDD), is an inspirational leader. Dr. Sylvio Dupuis, who was Insurance Commissioner when Tom took over Delta Dental in 1995, described Tom to me as "inspirational, out-of-the-box, forward-thinking, competent and honest." As you will learn as you read this book, Tom is a man with a passion for excellence who has thought deeply about what is required for long-term success. I have often heard him say, "Success is the sum of paying attention to detail," and that is exactly how he lives his life. You could call it his mantra.

Northeast Delta Dental retains 97 percent of its business every year, a remarkable feat when you consider the national rate of retention for medical and dental insurance customers is 80 percent. This is accomplished because Tom adheres rigorously to the golden rule of excellence in customer service. By internalizing the Baldrige principles of performance excellence (which you'll read more about in this book), Tom has improved processes and policies to improve service to customers. By fanatic adherence to these practices, Tom has grown the business and made Northeast Delta Dental a great place to work. *Business New Hampshire Magazine* selected NEDD as the best place to work in the years 1998, 1999, 2000, 2001, and 2002, after which they retired the company from the competition and Tom became a judge.

When Tom took the helm at NEDD, the company had seventy-five employees and most people in Northern New England had never heard of it. Now it's a household name and grown to the point where there are over 200 employees.

Under Tom's guidance, those with dental coverage in Northern New England have grown from 301,000 people in 1995 when Tom started at NEDD to over 750,000 in 2013. Northeast Delta Dental and Tom have

1

played a big role in making this happen. Using a low-profile campaign, they have helped mobilize dentists and built an innovative system with flexible products that has made it possible for many, many more people to have access to affordable dental coverage. One by one, they have extended dental benefits to people heretofore uncovered. Their efforts have improved dental health, overall health, and changed lives throughout the three New England states they serve.

Tom and the Delta Dental Plan of New Hampshire Board organized the Northeast Delta Dental Foundation, which puts part of the company's profits back into the community in support of good oral health. A good example of this is the Medicaid oral health program. Kids who qualified for this Medicaid program, including my own two grandchildren, were issued Delta Dental cards so they could seek treatment from 90 percent of the dentists in New Hampshire. Only one other state, Michigan, has anything remotely like this program. In a three-year period, Delta Dental contributed $1.5 million to supplement the program so 12,000 children could receive treatment. Every time Orion and Ariel smile at me, I think of Tom.

Tom and Northeast Delta Dental are known for their outstanding record of voluntary service to the community. At any given time, Tom is a member of more than a dozen civic boards and committees. It looks to me like Tom serves or has served on one-third of all the voluntary boards in the state. In fact, he chairs or has chaired one out of two boards on which he has served. He is much more than a name on a list; he truly gets involved. As someone told me, he takes on assignments and he delivers on them. Tom does not serve alone. Delta Dental managers serve on about sixty not-for-profit boards in New Hampshire.

Tom is well known for working long hours to achieve his vision for Northeast Delta Dental, its staff, customers and community. Although he sometimes compensates by cutting out a little early on a few winter weekdays to get some quality time skiing with his wife and children, he always seems to be accessible to those who need him. One of my favorite stories about Tom is told by two board members returning from a Saturday night Red Sox game. As they neared Concord, one joked that Tom was probably at his desk. After making a friendly wager, they called his direct line at the office. Guess who answered the phone?

– Lew Feldstein
President, New Hampshire Charitable Foundation
1986–2010

Game-changing Connection with Dave Cowens (Big Red)

For many years, based on my experience as a CEO, I contemplated writing a book on how to sustain business vitality over the long run. Northeast Delta Dental, I recognized early on, has the advantage of not being driven by Wall Street or short-term profitability. We are Main Street, which means that we can focus on doing what is best for all our stakeholder communities without the quarterly constraints imposed by shareholders.

With lots of support and wisdom from board members, such as Alan Brennan and Jane Kirk, and mentors, such as Dr. Sylvio Dupuis, Bob Dastin and Lew Feldstein, my colleagues at Northeast Delta Dental, and from the many CEOs of role model national and local companies who participated with me on leadership panels, I have developed a number of rules of thumb for long-term, sustained success. Then, about ten years ago, I began to assemble my thoughts and experiences into a file in preparation for writing this book.

I developed chapter themes and together with Barbara McLaughlin began the writing process. Barbara has been my right hand, my trusted confidante and my loyal and devoted teammate at Northeast Delta Dental since 1987, and I am forever grateful to her. As we moved forward, I jotted down ideas for the book, then we discussed them while Barbara captured my musings on paper. She edited and organized the ideas and eloquently brought our book to life.

Barbara and I felt pretty good about what we had produced and were ready to think of publishing, when I had a fortuitous meeting with former Boston Celtics great, Dave Cowens, in February of 2011 at an insurance conference where he was a keynote speaker. For the few readers who may not know about Dave, he was voted the most valuable player of the National Basketball Association (NBA) in the 1972-73 season and is a Hall of Fame basketball player who has received countless well-earned awards. (You can read more about him and his many accomplishments at the end of this book.)

I am a huge Boston Celtics fan as well as a Dave Cowens fan from the time he played a pick-up basketball game with a bunch of high school freshmen — including me — in a Weston, Massachusetts gymnasium back in 1970. I had admired his hustle and skill on the professional court throughout his career, so I was excited to hear Dave speak at the conference. I imagined tales of Celtics lore about famous coach and general manager Red Auerbach and about the 1974 and 1976 championships that Dave was instrumental in achieving.

I was surprised Dave's talk was more filled with inspirational and success factors than sports anecdotes. Dave emphasized the commonality of critical success factors in sports and business, and a repeating theme in his presentation was "do the right thing at the right time for the right reason."

The broad topics of Dave's talk paralleled the chapter headings of the book that Barbara and I had been writing. For instance, Dave's talk and our book both covered the importance of communication, teamwork, playing all out, earning trust and having the highest standards of performance. Really, the similarities were uncanny. Equally uncanny, Barbara had already given our manuscript the sports theme title of "There Are No Do-Overs."

Immediately following his talk, I approached Dave and remarked how there was consistency between success factors in sports and in business. I asked him, at this initial meeting, whether he would consider co-authoring a book with me on long-term business sustainability, as Dave's principles were so similar to mine, and all of them related to long-term vitality.

I had a few days left at the conference and used them to win him over. I outlined the values-driven, goal-driven approaches that we had used so successfully at Northeast Delta Dental, and it became clear that successful sports teams and sports franchises follow the same guiding principles as successful companies.

Dave described the need for integrity in relationships and the importance of leading by example. He described how legendary coach and general manager Red Auerbach and Hall of Famer John Havlicek led their lives as examples to the entire Celtics franchise. As he talked, I thought about the parallels for Northeast Delta Dental where one of our core values is integrity as the cornerstone of relationships with our employees, customers and communities.

Dave also described how hard he worked as a young college player and then later as an emerging NBA star, and that one of his skill sets was his ability to outwork other players. As I listened to Dave, I was thinking that outworking the competition was one of the key traits of successful companies and CEOs. My own company, Northeast Delta Dental, is, at its core, a regional company with only one major product (group dental insurance) and one mission focus (spreading affordable oral healthcare) competing against much larger, multi-line national insurance commercial carriers. As such, Northeast Delta Dental also has to outwork and outhustle formidable competition to be successful. In my mind, I could see the parallel of Dave outhustling Oscar Robertson for a loose ball in a 1974 NBA Championship game versus the Milwaukee Bucks, and Northeast Delta Dental outhustling companies such as Cigna or Anthem to become amazingly successful.

Dave and I continued to meet and exchange ideas over the next several months, and it was obvious that Dave was a man of the highest integrity, that he valued human relationships, and that he understood that quality starts at home. The more we talked, the more we realized that we agreed on the elements of sustained success and on Dave's personal mantra of "Do the right thing at the right time for the right reason."

Finally, after a lunch where Barbara and I met with Dave and his wife, Deby, Dave was finally convinced to join our book team. He became an integral part of the book writing process, and I will forever be grateful. In fact, when I was struggling to complete this book, Dave reminded me that telling my story is important because we are sharing real world experiences that work long term in business and in sports.

Game Plan: How We Organized the Book for You

Dave, Barbara, and I believe that, in business and in sports, it is vital to "do the right thing, at the right time, for the right reason," because in business and in sports you only get one shot to do it right! There are no do-overs. We believe that doing it right, on the first try, requires not just one skill but many. Just as a basketball player cannot succeed with just a layup or a free-throw shot or with just great ball handling or rebounding, so businesspeople need to develop several skill sets.

We organized this book around the principles that both Dave and I developed independently, but that are consistent with our business and sports experiences. We think the similarities between successful sports franchises and successful businesses will amaze you. We organized the skill sets into the book's chapters and then grouped the chapters following the four-quarter structure of an NBA game. We did this to emphasize the connection between sports and business and hope you find this memorable. Finally, we have used chapter titles that also carry out that theme. Each chapter begins with a story, in Dave's own words, about an experience in his career that illustrates the theme of the chapter. Then I share examples from my business experience. Each chapter ends with what we call a Big Red Factor that summarizes the keys to success detailed in the chapters.

What is a Big Red Factor? One of Dave's nicknames on the court in his playing days was "Big Red," given to him by the famous radio voice of the Boston Celtics, Johnny Most, who called play-by-play for nearly all of the Celtics dynasty years. Dave had red hair and, at six-foot, nine-inches, was on the smaller side for a professional NBA center. Johnny Most gave Dave Cowens the nickname, "Big Red," in spite of his size but because of his big impact on the game, and it stuck. So, as we were constructing this book and thinking about Dave's contributions, we thought — let's call these long-term success principles "Big Red Factors."

Finally, no book written by Boston Celtics fans would be complete without a sprinkling of wise quotes from wise people, including Celtics coach Red Auerbach, who influenced many generations of players and businesspeople.

The Draft and Preseason Workouts

"Just do what you do best."
                                    – Red Auerbach

Chapter 1

Find the Right Players for the Right Positions

*"One man can be a crucial ingredient on a team,
but one man cannot make a team."*

– Kareem Abdul-Jabbar

*Long before I was awarded a four-year basketball scholarship to
Florida State University in 1966, my high school coach told me if I was
five feet away from the basket with the ball, I should pass it out to a
guard and not shoot. When I advanced to the Celtics, I was lucky to play
alongside Larry Bird. Larry was an offensive genius and as competitive
and dedicated to his coach as any athlete has ever been. His ability to
control games was on a level enjoyed by only a few others. So, if someone
passed me the ball to shoot, I would pass and defer to Bird; Bird only had
God to pass to who would have a higher chance of making the winning
shot.*

*Perhaps I didn't have the best shot, but I was fortunate to be born
with a certain amount of athleticism, and what I recognized early on in
my formative years was my ability to jump, rebound, and play with an*

unbridled source of energy. I didn't need to have the best shot — at least not at first. In the beginning, corralling missed shots was my ticket to success. I worked with that to develop myself into a stronger, more reliable, and more resilient overall athlete. I became adept in finding ways to capitalize on the combination of physical abilities given to me through birth and the energy and hard work of honing my skill level to excel.

My playing career at Florida State University was highlighted by three years of continual improvement as a player and as a part of a team. I was the MVP of the team all three varsity years. My rebounding records still stand because today's style of play doesn't produce enough missed shots that lead to rebounds.

During my senior year, we played in Dayton, Ohio against the Dayton Flyers. I heard there were a few NBA scouts in attendance, most notably Red Auerbach of the Celtics. I have heard the story that he made a big show of leaving early and shaking his head in disgust to show the other scouts there that he did not think any player in the game was a potential NBA pick, knowing full well he wanted me. He selected me as the fourth pick in the first round a month or so later during the annual NBA draft. Only Pete Maravich, Bob Lanier and Rudy Tomjanovich were selected before me.

It seems to me that the sooner a person realizes what his or her true strengths are, the sooner he or she can concentrate on perfecting that trait to the point that other talents can be developed to complement his or her primary strength.

Know yourself with an objective mindset. Constant self-analysis is a healthy exercise.

– Dave Cowens

Big Red figured out what he could do better than anyone else on the basketball court. It is the same with business. Those at the helm of companies have to determine how to develop an environment where employees understand what they do better than anyone else in the company. As the famous author Jim Collins conveys in his widely acclaimed book, *Good to Great*, having the right people in the right seats on the bus is one of the keys to an organization's success. This mantra goes back to Teddy Roosevelt who said, "The best executive is the one who has sense enough to pick good men [and women] to do what he [she] wants done, and self-restraint to keep from meddling with them while they do it."

Everyone has an important position in the company, be it in the mailroom, executive management, marketing department or boardroom. And while every position is significant, it is important to recognize that every position is different, and for a good reason and purpose. Going back to Collins' bus analogy, the leader of an organization must make sure that everybody is truly on board with the organization's mission or purpose, and more importantly, each person on the bus is sitting in the right seat.

My own example that parallels Dave's occurred in 1995, when I was recruited at age thirty-eight to come to Northeast Delta Dental (NEDD) as its CEO. I asked an insurance colleague, Al Breitman, what he thought. He said something I have never forgotten, "Don't consider a new position until you are ready and have the skills for the position." As it turns out, they offered me the job at NEDD as I was driving back to Massachusetts from

> **Everyone has an important position in the company, be it in the mailroom...or the boardroom.**

my interview (they called me on my mobile phone, then an analog bag phone in my car). I accepted and soon learned NEDD was a perfect fit for my executive skill set — the willingness to go out in the community and make a difference, the ability to provide an inspirational "total quality" boost to a solid company, and the persuasive ability to transition the culture to encourage employee empowerment.

The crux of my management style is that the leadership team and all our teammates do a self-analysis to understand their abilities. This helps make it clear what job contribution each member is most qualified to do: the job that one employee can do better than anyone else. For example, if I am an extroverted salesperson who could sell ice in Antarctica, I need to make it clear to my boss, and my boss needs to understand and accept, that the one thing I do better than anyone else is sell. This is my job and my best fit for maximum contribution. The exemplary superstar salesperson must feel comfortable that he or she is best suited to sales, and the management team can acknowledge that fact and reward the salesperson for being the best salesperson.

Promoting the salesperson as a reward to a position that is not what that person does best may be moving him or her to the wrong seat on the bus. Management and employees must be willing to have honest, ongoing dialogue and mutual trust, so promotions occur that benefit both the employee and the company. If the manager promotes that salesperson to a job that no longer fits that person's capabilities, it will be to the detriment of the employee, the employee's colleagues and the company.

It is first important to hire the right person in order to get the right people on the bus. Under the leadership of our award-winning Vice President of Human Resources, Connie Roy-Czyzowski, we have developed an elaborate hiring process that takes into consideration three critical success factors:

- Is the potential candidate a critical thinker?

- Does he or she have interpersonal communication skills to be an effective team player?

- Does that person have the self-integrity to know and ask for the position that is the best fit?

If a company hires the right people and has the right policies and procedures, there is no need to micro-manage them. Once they are trained, understand their goals, have a good idea as to what is expected of them and feel comfortable, only then do employees become truly empowered. They make the right decisions as they see them, and they make these decisions with the confidence that they have the support of management and other employees. The only exception might be in an emergency or a company-changing situation, such as a major IT systems conversion or a crisis, when employees quickly look to expert leaders for direction.

Like Northeast Delta Dental, your company can create a culture where skilled and trained employees are able to enhance their work by sharing their best ideas on how to improve things. This can happen when:

- Employees believe they are well qualified because of the intrinsic training you have provided.

- You create idea-sharing systems that encourage employees to share their best ideas on ways to improve the company.

It is interesting that the right employees with the right skills are willing to propose improvement ideas, even if it means employees may "idea" themselves out of a job. They feel comfortable doing this because they know the company recognizes their skills and will move them to other positions where they can contribute.

This works because the best companies have employees who trust management. Risk-taking employees understand ideas better the company and may create new opportunities for themselves within another department or a new job that takes advantage of their expertise.

In his book, *Ideas Are Free*, Dr. Alan G. Robinson's overarching point is that the company must have a culture where ideas flow freely in order for the company to perform as well as possible. At Northeast Delta Dental, our idea program flourishes because those who do the work submit their suggestions for improvements. Management quickly responds back to the idea person either with approval for implementation of the idea, a reward or an explanation why we cannot implement the idea (for example, until the NEDD Board provides approval for an expenditure related to the idea). Sometimes we simply cannot implement an idea, but the submitter receives an explanation as to why not. The keys are that employees know we want ideas to flow freely and that we know and trust them to do their jobs. The parallel to sports is that companies with the right players in the right positions have men and women who are confident enough to be team players.

Every human being wants to be the best he or she can be. The responsibility of your organization is to be sure that each person is filling a position for which he or she is qualified and for which he or she has passion. If leadership is committed to the notion that every position is equally important and slots employees in the right seat on the bus, the organization will flourish. It is also the responsibility of the employees to recognize what they can do better than anyone else can and to leverage those unique skill sets. As employees, we have to figure out how are we unique. What sets us apart? As the company, we have to create a culture where employees are poised for success by developing opportunities in which they share a stake in the outcome.

It is impossible for any one person in the company to do every job in the company, just as it was impossible for Dave Cowens or Larry Bird to play all five positions on the basketball team. But Dave's or Larry's coach, like a CEO or management team, should be able to bring out the best in individual players by fostering a team culture. Keeping this type of person on your sports team or in your corporation is paramount to establishing a winning team that will sustain its winning record.

THE BIG RED FACTOR

As a business leader, I have learned it is better to have no one in the job than to have the wrong person in the job. As Jim Collins discovered when researching his book *Good to Great*, "when in doubt, don't hire – keep looking." We look for people with the skills we need, and we prepare them to be able to offer their best performance. We want them to want to come to work every day. We want them to enjoy their positions and make use of their strengths with confidence. We want them to feel that they are an important part of a winning team. And we want them to feel comfortable enough to offer ideas for how the team can become even stronger.

Chapter 2

Develop Your Players' Skills

"Success is that place in the road where
preparation meets opportunity."

– Branch Rickey

All through my basketball career, I learned from coaching and repetition. But I also sought out ways to become a better player that were not commonplace. As odd as it may seem, weight training was frowned upon prior to the mid-seventies. When I graduated from high school I was 6´- 6˝, weighed 190 pounds and was soon playing in scrimmages against 6´- 10˝, 250-pound players on my Florida State University college varsity team. Even though I was able to jump with them and "out quick" them, they were stronger and heavier and tougher to move around.

Then I ran into a guy who lifted weights in our small college dorm weight room (one bench, some barbells, pulleys on the wall, a sit-up rack). I asked him if he would teach me how to properly lift for basketball, and he worked out with me my first spring. That summer and three consecutive summers during the off-season, I went back home, kept lifting three times a week, played ball five times a week, and held down various labor jobs.

Over time, I developed a physique that allowed me to compete with bigger and stronger players. Being committed to weight training gave me an upper hand at the end of my college days with the pro scouts. My head coach also noticed and urged other players to use a similar routine.

– Dave Cowens

In business, as in sports, we all face the question of when to take a risk or try something new to develop a person's talents. Just as Dave did when he tried weight training, then a very unconventional approach, many of us have to decide what we need to build our skills or the skills of our colleagues. In my career, I took a risk in 1985 when I moved from a solid position at John Hancock (a large commercial carrier with headquarters in Boston) to Delta Dental of Massachusetts (DDMA), a startup company with no infrastructure, no facility and no employees but only contracts on paper with customers and dentists. They hired me as the operations head to recruit 100+ employees and set up systems, a claims office, and design a building in order for DDMA to be a stand-alone company. We had nine months to accomplish this — a real life MBA project, while I was completing my MBA during the evenings at Babson College.

I am thankful for this start-up experience of DDMA, which positioned me to be CEO of Northeast Delta Dental (NEDD) ten years later. I had literally done every job at DDMA, so very little surprised me once I arrived at NEDD. I had done it all — from the mailroom to systems to marketing — which enhanced my credibility among NEDD employee colleagues. (At NEDD we use the term "employee colleague" instead of "employee," to emphasize the respect we have at all levels of our organization. However, for this book, we will use the simpler "employee" or "colleague.") I recognize a leader does not have to have a total grasp of each employee's position description, but my understanding of positions in a dental insurance company certainly helped me be an empathetic leader and an effective coach. In fact, there is no doubt that my previous experience helped as I mentored and coached my colleagues at NEDD.

17

As CEO, just as if I were a coach, my job is to create the vision, develop the strategic game plan and create the environment where colleagues can thrive. My job is to ensure that all of our employees understand our mission and their role in it, and have the training, coaching and confidence to do their jobs well. No amount of external speeches, no volume of inspirational blogs, no number of successful board meetings would make a hill of beans difference if our dentists weren't receiving their checks, if our subscribers weren't receiving their explanations of benefits, if group purchasers weren't receiving their monthly invoices on time, or if our call center was slow or nonresponsive in any way. So, how do I make sure employees do all these jobs, and do them well, if speeches or pep talks alone are not enough?

A hallmark of the companies that are selected as the best places to work as well as the most successful sports franchises are the opportunities for employees to learn and develop new skills and to progress and advance within the organization as their performance and desires dictate. We at Northeast Delta Dental, just like the Celtics, provide lots of training and mentoring. This kind of active support is why we have repeatedly won awards as one of the best places to work.

First, we regularly determine what training employees need. We study staff performance reviews, talk to managers and even ask the employees what they want to learn. Then we develop a training plan. (Sounds a lot like what good coaches do, doesn't it?)

Some of the courses we provide include dental terminology, our IT system, leadership, communication, team building and analytical and core business skills. We also provide all training needed for our employees to gain and maintain their professional licenses and certifications. Over time, we have built up a substantial library of books, as well as audio and video materials. When employees told us they wanted to learn how to speak in public, we set up a Toastmasters group for them. We offer tuition reimbursement for college courses and continuing education credits for employees with professional designations. There are many other external educational possibilities — professional development workshops, online classes, leadership enrichment programs — to encourage continued learning, no matter how much education we have already.

Realizing that managers need to be good mentors and coaches, we provide future managers with supervisory skill building training — available internally or externally. We train our managers to understand the generational and cultural differences among our staff and to use their skills to be consistent but use situational leadership versus a cookie-cutter approach when dealing with people. We teach them that they need to be coaches and mentors, not autocrats. Whatever one's background, whatever race, gender, age, religion or disability they may have, people want their managers and coworkers to treat them with respect and know that they matter in a work environment. They want their voices to be heard.

A final step in our education or training is to monitor how we are doing. We track how much training people get (for instance, our customer service representatives take an average of 300 hours of on-the-job training before they get on the phone with customers) as well as how effective our training is.

Our training or education is not unlike a university. Creating an environment where human beings can thrive is a critical success factor that transcends all industries and organizations. Look at the emerging nationally acclaimed High Point University (HPU) in High Point, North Carolina. Its president, Dr. Nido Qubein, was born in the Middle East and came to the U.S. with little knowledge of the English language, but has accomplished great things. Among other triumphs (he has several published books and serves on many corporate boards), he has propelled the university to remarkable heights. President Qubein's approach at HPU is to provide students with the best infrastructure and the best professors and teachers. The idea is that the students can flourish, and that the students' "job" is to take advantage of the outstanding infrastructure, go to class and excel at their studies.

The HPU credo is to deliver educational experiences that enlighten, challenge and prepare students to lead lives of significance in complex global communities. Having a son, Brian, recently graduate from HPU, I can attest first hand that the HPU education fostered by President Qubein works well. Brian graduated with honors, is competent with life skills, is ready to be a leader — and has a job!

19

NEDD has a traditional tuition reimbursement program, and many employees have used this to earn their degrees through the years. Two success stories include Anders (Andy) Tabor and ex-colleague Gina Powers. Andy Tabor, a big Yankees fan, now has his associate's degree in sports management from the New Hampshire Technical Institute (NHTI). He found the experience worthwhile even though it took him almost nine years to complete because he took only one class per semester. The day Andy graduated from NHTI I had the honor of handing him his diploma, as I was a commencement speaker at the graduation that day. Recently, I presented Andy with his twenty-five year NEDD anniversary pin and Quarter Century Club plaque at our All Colleagues Meeting, and then recognized several employees, who, like Andy, effectively used our tuition reimbursement program. Andy now uses his sports management degree, as his position at NEDD now includes coordinating our event tickets and assisting at NEDD's special external events.

Another success story is Gina Powers. She worked full time in the data entry department at Northeast Delta Dental by day and attended college in the evening, working tirelessly on her Bachelor of Science degree in criminal justice at Franklin Pierce University, taking one or two courses at a time. After moving to California, Gina continued her studies, eventually achieving her master's in forensic science. She then began her career at the Yolo County, California Sheriff's Department as a Deputy Coroner. Gina says, "The financial stress of paying for college was relieved by the knowledge that Northeast Delta Dental would be there to help me out. It was nice to be able to take courses that were not related to my employment at the time, as it was clear my educational goals and career path were in the field of criminal justice and law enforcement." Gina was a dedicated and loyal employee at Northeast Delta Dental for seven years and strongly encourages folks to take advantage of the program. Her continuing career success all began while she was at Northeast Delta Dental!

A third example is from former colleague Maryanne Aldrich who writes:

"I can't believe it has been over five years since I left the NEDD organization; I still speak to some former colleagues and enjoy the annual holiday cards with a personalized note. It always reminds me why NEDD is such a gold standard in the workforce and how much I miss all of you! Though I am still enjoying the change I made to become a Community Relations Director for Cottage Hospital, I utilize the skills I gained while at NEDD and am happy to report that I just finished my MBA program through Plymouth State; I credit NEDD for giving me the start on that educational journey."

Gina's and Maryanne's stories demonstrate our belief that when an employee advances and achieves a degree, that is to our advantage as a success story. When an employee moves to a position outside of NEDD,

Mentors are leaders who prompt us to do our best so that we make our dreams for our future a reality.

we call these outside of NEDD "promotions." So, for example, when an employee leaves and we do our customary farewell party celebrating their departure, we view this as a success for the employee and the company. If you think of it, if one of your best employees has earned a degree through your tuition reimbursement, s/he is incredibly motivated and loyal to the company. One example of this was an employee who left, became a Human Resources VP, and ended up purchasing dental insurance from us. Even if an employee leaves the firm, the goodwill and knowledge that we made that person's life better is a reward in itself. Our tuition reimbursement program is a perfect example of "doing the right thing, at the right time, for the right reason."

In addition to training and education, we at Northeast Delta Dental believe in mentoring. Good companies like ours don't just hire you or even just train you. They keep developing you. We are looking for employees who are eager to learn and who want to work for the kind of company that will help them grow. We look for employees who appreciate the value of learning, who think critically and who communicate clearly. These disciplines are invaluable for a lifetime.

Mentors are leaders who prompt us to do our best so that we make our dreams for our future a reality. When it comes to mentoring, NEDD does not have a formal internal mentor program because our informal system seems to work well. Family members and close friends are often our first mentors. There are many CEOs who have become friends and who serve on panels with me. Most of us talk about the importance of being a mentor and a mentee. My co-author and close colleague, Barbara McLaughlin, and I have mentored each other through the years together, and she has mentored nearly a dozen other colleagues who have risen to the top.

Within NEDD, we emphasize supportive relationships that will help our colleagues become strong leaders. Mentoring is a team of two. We are looking for employees who are willing to work in teams to meet business objectives. As mentees, they are likely to be involved with their mentors and others to continue to enhance their abilities. I encourage everyone to develop a mentoring relationship. A good mentor can direct the mentee to many of the resources needed to be successful and confident and may help him or her avoid making costly mistakes.

As a coach, some of the greatest highlights of my professional career derive from the professional development of employees and business colleagues whom I have mentored. I have valued my mentors, giants in New Hampshire such as Dr. Sylvio Dupuis and Brigadier General (RET) Robert Dastin, so it was only natural for me to reach out to younger colleagues and become a mentor.

My first mentees at NEDD were Julie Nieder and Jodie Hittle, two younger up-and-coming employees destined for leadership positions. I would meet regularly with Julie and Jodie, and we developed five-year professional development plans, including milestones involving educational goals, training goals, career goals, and work/family goals. Jodie started in the Concord home office mailroom, was promoted to the market manager of NEDD's Maine territory, and eventually reached our mutual goal when he was promoted to vice president of sales and marketing. Julie's employment history was also filled with a series of promotions, ultimately culminating in a director-level position responsible for major system testing, an extremely important position in an insurance company such as NEDD.

Mentoring young women professionals is an important role for any business leader. A publication by the New Hampshire Women's Policy Institute, "Breaking Through the Granite Ceiling in Corporate New Hampshire" (2008), documented how glass-ceiling barriers are preventing women executives from reaching top management in New Hampshire. As noted in this study, "Women in New Hampshire comprise 47 percent of the workforce, 61 percent of recent college graduates, and just over half of the state's managers and professionals, but represent a minority of those serving on governing boards and in executive positions." My goal is to break down these barriers in the corporate world by being a mentor to women executives and by proactively increasing the gender balance on boards on which I serve and in the composition of NEDD's own boards.

We have also recognized that being comfortable on the golf course has business advantages. This is one reason why NEDD continues to be the major sponsor of the only LPGA sanctioned golf tournament in northern New England. The professional players put on clinics for women executives to learn or to improve their golf game.

Outside of the company, Northeast Delta Dental supports programs that offer strong mentorship components for students and future business leaders. Teachers and business and community leaders are natural, influential mentors. For example, we made a three-year financial and mentoring commitment in Manchester, New Hampshire to City Year New Hampshire. (City Year New Hampshire is an innovative, education-focused, nonprofit, public-private partnership that helps public schools keep students in school and on track to graduate.) The support of fifty-six mentors acting as tutors and role models helped City Year to expand the program from one Manchester school to five. With the backing of Northeast Delta Dental, I have also been personally very excited to be involved with the 140 business leaders who support the New Hampshire Scholars Initiative by making classroom presentations, offering job-shadowing opportunities, serving on advisory groups and advisory boards and participating in mentoring sessions.

THE BIG RED FACTOR

The best organizations routinely offer opportunities for ongoing learning and development. They also make an effort to encourage employees to take advantage of these opportunities to develop their skills and enhance their value to the organization and their chances for a better future for themselves and their families. In Dave's case, he sought out ways to improve his skills, and his learning eventually helped other players when the coach saw the value of weight training. In an ideal world, maximizing a player's or employee's skills is a combined effort on the part of both the organization and the individual. As Big Red himself says, "It's an organization's responsibility to create the opportunity and an employee's responsibility to seize it."

Chapter 3

Keep the Team Healthy

"Be strong in body, clean in mind, lofty in ideals."

– James Naismith

All the coaches I played for — which includes me — had different philosophies on scrimmages, practice schedules, the organization of team drills, on how to teach, and on the use of individual time for skills improvement on fundamentals such as footwork, free throw shooting, and conditioning.

I believe most college coaches consistently run practices by breaking down each training segment into five to fifteen minute time periods. They adhere to that start and stop time process, except perhaps at tournament time when they will change their training routine in response to travel and game times or to prepare for the unique challenges of the opposing team.

Pro coaches are a bit more flexible and run over scheduled training time periods if they feel it's necessary. It often depends on which part of the season it is. Training camp routines are much different than mid-season. The professional practice varies as well because the professionals play an average of three games a week for six months with half of them being on the road. Therefore, many times rest and mental preparation have higher priority than an actual workout in the gym.

All in all, the experienced coaches always keep in mind that it's the performance in the game that matters most and that everything that's done during the course of a season is to maximize the effort and performance of the players during the game.

Coaches walk a fine line between getting the team ready for competition and mentally burning them out or making them so fatigued physically that they become what we call leg weary. Coaches know that players respond to well considered, concise, and meaningful practice sessions. If players feel as though a coach is wasting their time by over-talking, by not adhering to a defined schedule, or by working on things that are inane then the coach will not earn their respect. Players actually like to practice, but they hate it when a coach wastes their time.

Injuries occur all the time. Sometimes a player arrives at the start of the season with an old injury or one he incurred over the off-season. Everyone takes precautions and thinks about how much is too much. Not all players have the same tolerances for playing through pain. Not all injuries lead directly to more serious damage to the body. As an athlete, you have to embrace pain in order to condition yourself adequately for the demands of your sport. Repetition is necessary but that leads to wear and tear. Players, the team doctor and the training staff (but not the coach or management) make the decisions on whether or not a player is healthy enough to practice or play in a game.

Most teams have strength and conditioning gurus to monitor players' activities that are specific to their sport. Weight training to maintain overall body strength throughout the season and during the off-season has turned into a science. Stretching, nutrition, sleep patterns, hydration, warm-up routines, meditation, rehab techniques, food supplementation, etc. are part of the sports scene nowadays and have taken on a high level of importance due to the sizable investment in players and what is at stake financially and spiritually for players and teams in winning championships or titles.

– Dave Cowens

Northeast Delta Dental (NEDD) has won many awards for its best practices in keeping its employees fit, happy, healthy and productive. The award we are proudest of is being selected as one of the 25 Best Small Companies to Work for in America in 2004, 2005, 2006, 2007 and 2008. That means that the Great Place to Work® Institute and the Society for Human Resource Management ranked us among the nation's best for five years running! We did not win this award by accident or good luck; we won it through concentrated hard work on something we believe in — taking care of our people and creating a high trust environment at work.

I have had the opportunity to serve on many panels with CEOs of companies that are employers of choice. All of these CEOs and their organizations believe in the importance of keeping our teams fit and healthy because they know that a healthy team is a high-performing team. We all may do things a bit differently, but let me share with you some of the practices we use at NEDD:

- Flexible work schedules

- Work from home

- Four free personal days annually for non-exempt employees in addition to earned time

- Our VIP program (Volunteer Involvement Pays), which is paid time off to volunteer

- Time to serve on boards/advisory groups

- Employee Community Involvement Grant, which encourages employees to apply for a grant for their favorite charity

• Blending of community related projects at work

• Generous time off policies

• Holidays off plus occasional special Delta Dental holidays

• Employer-matched fundraisers

• Safety net benefits provided, such as short- and long-term disability insurance, life insurance and pension/401k plans

• Access to free financial advisor

• Retirement seminars

• Fitness center/fitness programs

•Informative Lunch & Learn programs

• Health and safety teams that conduct ergonomic and fire inspections and train first responders on the use of defibrillators (AEDs)

• Health screenings and flu shots

• Free fresh fruit daily

• Great medical, dental, and vision plans (with dental and vision 100 percent paid)

Allow me to describe just a few of these practices in more detail. We work hard at NEDD, but we also respect time with family. It is important that an organization's policies, practices and culture respect the fact that employees have lives outside work and affirmatively help them balance the competing demands of work and family. The CEO must walk the talk when it comes to a work-life balance. Anybody coaching or mentoring people in the company must be genuine about promoting the work-life balance — this includes telecommuting. We have well-documented policies that promote flexible schedules, and we train our managers and supervisors on these policies as part of our culture. We do this because we want to avoid a situation where a manager might give an employee requested time off but might demonstrate annoyance with the request through negative body language. This could create cultural confusion, which we want to avoid. It could tell employees that the person who gets ahead is the one who works all the time and does not

> **The best companies...affirm the need to balance work and family demands and keep them in harmony.**

request time off. We want all our cultural signals to be in alignment because the informal mechanisms and service culture are actually more important in the implementation of the work-life balance than the written rules.

While Americans pride ourselves on always being connected with our iPads, iPhones and other portable devices, corporate America could no doubt learn from Western Europe. European employees take long vacations with their families during their summer months, and they leave work at work. Think about it: when you meet people in the United States, they tend to talk first about what they do for work. In Europe, people generally talk about their families first.

Understanding the need for work/life balance and providing help to employees in balancing the competing demands of work and family life can pay off. The best employers structure policies and practices in a way that respects the fact that employees have lives outside of work. The best companies proactively affirm the need to balance work and family demands and keep them in harmony.

I have found that encouraging people to work from home works well for certain positions in the company. For example, External Affairs employees need quiet time to write broker/customer newsletters and annual reports, and thus they are actually more productive at home.

Conversely, though our insurance world communicates more and more through electronic means with over 70 percent of our dental claims submitted electronically, still 30 percent of our claims come in via the United States Postal Service in hardcopy form. Therefore, it is important that folks in the mailroom be in the office to physically open envelopes and move the claims onward.

We try to explain to all our employees that some positions are better suited to work from home while others require physical presence in the office. We have also learned from study and analysis that those who wish to work from home miss the "water cooler" talk and the day-to-day interaction with other adults who have respect for you and your job. Many employees tell me at the informal Coffee with the Coach get-togethers that coming to work for NEDD is a wonderful escape from the stress of their home life.

My advice for employers who are planning to implement work-from-home policies is that you categorize positions to know which ones can optionally and optimally work from home, and which cannot. Also, recognize that even those who work from home do require occasional face-time in the office to maintain the cultural connection.

At NEDD, we are committed to the idea that we should celebrate lifestyle and individual passions. In order to respect and celebrate what most fundamentally drives a person, we offer paid time off for employees who volunteer in the community. Many of our employees volunteer at soup kitchens, churches and synagogues, their local schools, or favorite charities. We try not to let these folks go unrecognized, so we have a "VIP" program that helps make the volunteer process more transparent. It actually encourages people who may not have thought to volunteer to go out and do so with paid time away from the office. All we ask in return is that each VIP recipient talks about his or her experience at our quarterly All Colleagues Meetings and prepare a write-up to publish in our internal newsletter, *Team Power*. Enjoying the community and serving on not-for-profit boards or advisory groups allows employees to grow professionally. Those employees bring their learning experiences back into the workplace and they become better employees as a result.

We think community engagement is win-win: it benefits not only society at-large but also the employer. The employee now has a broader perspective on life. Not-for-profit community organizations gain NEDD's governance and fundraising expertise, and NEDD is rewarded with more worldly employees. My colleague, Lew Feldstein, would be quick to add that getting involved with community organizations enhances society and makes the engaged citizen live longer.

In business as in sports, it is impossible to over-emphasize the importance of physical and mental health fitness. At NEDD, we have two on-site fitness centers along with running groups, walking groups, yoga groups, aerobics groups, a ski team, and a cross-country ski group. We attempt to give each employee the opportunity to remain fit doing the exercise of his or her choice. When we first opened our fitness center at NEDD in 2004, we had done research on the handful of other companies in New Hampshire that had fitness centers. We learned that the fitness centers employees used most heavily were ones that had a cheerleader, i.e., a certified fitness trainer who could demonstrate proper use of the equipment and who would encourage employees on their fitness path. Therefore, our fitness center includes a personal fitness trainer, Tom Walton, who is an expert at encouraging and motivating employees, whether they are elite athletes or simply aging adults trying to regain or retain good fitness.

Tom is, in fact, such a renowned coach that he was selected in 2013 for New Hampshire's highest award for volunteer service to youth in sports: the Carl A. Lundholm Memorial Award. Like me, employees consider Tom the coach around the NEDD campus, as he inspires and motivates employees to exercise, eat right and change their behaviors to live a healthier lifestyle.

In the same way you cannot have good overall health without good oral health, you cannot have wellness without mental health. Accordingly, we also offer an Employee Assistance Program and other life-coaching programs for employees who may be struggling with issues at home or who need professional development at the office.

A team's most valuable part is the reputation it has for consistently making players feel important, and feel that they are being treated fairly and like worthy individuals. I have seen some players who had reputations as malcontents join the Celtics and become ideal teammates because they recognized they were in a special situation. No one remembers the wins or losses as well as they remember the character of the people with whom they worked and lived. Their humor, strength, generosity, sharing, makes us all stronger in so many ways because it exposes our vulnerabilities and creates moments to learn and grow. Teams that support their players and help them remain healthy and productive without wearing them down are far more likely to succeed in the long run than those that treat players as expendable parts of a machine rather than as valued individuals.

THE BIG RED FACTOR

The best teams and employers tend to take care of their people first, encouraging work-life balance and good physical and mental health. They do this because they recognize that profitability follows when employees are satisfied and working in a supportive environment. NEDD is not about running a country club to keep employees happy. Rather, our way is to encourage the work-life balance and have employees feel good about themselves. We know this translates into better customer service, which in turn creates more opportunities within a successful company — a beautiful circle.

First Quarter

"Natural abilities are like natural plants; they need pruning by study."

– Red Auerbach

Chapter 4

Play All Out

"The harder you practice, the luckier you get."

– Golfer Jerry Barber

As an intern, I worked at a basketball camp at Davidson College in June 1969, for its famed coach, Charles "Lefty" Driesell. We had a staff that consisted of well-known players Pete Maravich, Charlie Scott, Bobby Cremins, Mike Maloy, Fox DeMoisey, a few players from the New York area and a few other Davidson players (Pete Maravich was a hall of famer, Charlie Scott played on the Celtics 1976 championship team, and Mike Maloy was the first African American to join a college fraternity at Davidson). We all made $40 for the week, plus room and board. Pete did a ball handling, dribbling and tricks lecture for an hour, and was paid $100. I paid close attention to Pete's lecture because I wanted to earn $100 an hour and not $40 per week. The rest of the summer I worked on all the dribbling and technical drills, and it made me a much more confident and trustworthy player because I could then dribble and pass *well for a big man.*

This addition to my game and the motivation of my shooting made me a well-rounded player that allowed the coach to feel confident in me no matter what the circumstances in the game. As a result, I got to play more minutes and got more rebound opportunities. The rest is history. But aside from all that, my trademark was one of attitude — hustling, diving on the floor out of bounds for a loose ball — that endeared me to fans and became my brand or symbol. For me a loose ball was just like a rebound but not as high in the air. It was like a free for all, first to it won. Now, the comment — and I believe it's a compliment — I get today from forty, fifty, sixty, seventy, and eighty-year-old people is one that focuses on my all-out play and not one particular skill. They tell me they appreciate that I was willing to do the work, to play all out.

– Dave Cowens

The very best athletes — Michael Jordan, Larry Bird, Magic Johnson — in addition to their extreme talents, worked longer and harder than their peers to become superior athletes and champions. Magic put in extra hours knowing Larry was doing the same. When Magic entered the NBA, he was not a great outside shooter or a league leading free-throw maker. Magic worked at it and became a 90+ percent free-throw player, demonstrating that even the best can get better.

As Dave reveals above, one of his major talents was consistent all-out play and out-hustling his competitors. Who can forget the 1974 and 1976 NBA playoffs when Dave's hustle forced a seven-game championship victory over the Milwaukee Bucks (with Oscar Robertson and Kareem Abdul-Jabbar) and a six-game championship victory over the Phoenix Suns, including the dramatic three-overtime Game 5 of the series?

When I am at speaking engagements and making presentations to college and MBA students, folks ask me the secret to my success. I always respond: work harder than anyone else. The fact is I am simply willing to do more than the average person — both to get the work done and to invest in making myself the best I can be. There are many facets of leaders in business, but one overarching theme is that the most successful businessperson outworks the competition. Each of us has unique talents, but what sets us apart is hard work. We may not be able to control our specific talents, but we can control how much effort we put forth. You can choose to buckle down for the long haul and apply yourself.

As a personal example, at the end of a normal workday, I often feel tired from endless meetings, memos and emails. But there still may be three potential customers who left voicemail or email messages, and expect to receive a return call or email. The successful businessperson will suck it up and make those three calls or emails before leaving for the day, albeit already a very long day. Before going home, I make those calls. I have many credos I impart to my NEDD colleagues, and one is, "Never put off until tomorrow what you can accomplish today." That is how to get ahead. There are no shortcuts in sports or business. If you want the big payoff, you need to put in the work.

As a NEDD-wide example, in 2004 we underwent a major information technology systems conversion. For almost an entire year, we expected employees to work six to seven days each week, and asked them to execute a flawless work and system transition plan. Flawless system conversions usually do not happen in the insurance and financial services industry. Flaws in the claims processing system result in unprocessed or inaccurately processed claims, incorrect check payments and calls that go unanswered or unreturned. Moreover, these flaws can quickly take down an insurance company, sometimes almost overnight. Have you ever received notices from your insurance company indicating that, due to a systems conversion, claims payments will be later than usual or that their call center response time will be slow? Have you received a communication from your bank that your statement may be incorrect due to a conversion? If you have received such notices, what did you think about the quality of that organization? Not much, I bet.

We knew we had to avoid these kinds of flaws because two of our culture's values are quality and teamwork. We explained all this to our employees, emphasizing the need for attention to detail and the need to work long and hard. We began by working to reduce our inventory of claims outstanding. That way, customers actually received better service immediately following the conversion. We used this inventory reduction strategy just in case the new system was behind schedule, and so inventory would float up to normal levels, instead of high levels. We never wanted to write letters to our customers or dentists that one so often sees that "we are experiencing high volumes of claims/phone calls during our system conversion, please accept our apologies."

Our biggest compliments were from customers and dental offices who said in early January, 2005 right after the conversion, "I thought you were doing a system conversion." In fact, we had, but the process was so seamless that not one customer experienced a hiccup in service. These customers were so used to rocky conversions from their other insurance companies or banks, that they were astounded with the flawlessness of our conversion.

We did not falter because employees understood why we were all working so hard. They believed in what we were asking them to do because we took the time to explain their role in the process. Because we communicated so thoroughly, employees understood their role. They saw the need to give extra, and clearly saw that a smooth systems conversion would be a critical strategic success factor for the corporation and would open doors to new opportunities for them.

What also happened in 2004 was that Northeast Delta Dental received an unheard of highest ranking in an employee climate survey. This was at a time when, ironically, one might have expected an opposite outcome due to the excessively long workweeks. None of this would have been possible if the employees throughout NEDD did not trust the leadership. At the same time, the leadership team had to trust that the people were excited to come into work every day and do their jobs efficiently and effectively. It is no surprise, then, that our major system conversion was flawless.

One of the two founders of Paul Mitchell systems, John Paul DeJoria, who is now a billionaire, notes, "The difference between successful people and unsuccessful people is the successful people do all the things the unsuccessful people don't want to do." Substitute "company" for "people" and that is the major secret of Northeast Delta Dental. All employees, not just the CEO, are willing to delight the customer by making that one last call before going home, by responding quickly to each customer request and by taking steps to be an expert in dental insurance to ensure customers get not only a timely answer but a correct answer.

Although this is a straightforward formula, few organizations follow it because it is difficult and costly. There are now economic incentives to have automated customer service call centers, with auto attendants and frustrating navigation software. NEDD's formula will remain the human touch, while having the best technology and social media for our younger customers who, based on research, want some answers without talking to a human being. Yet, to this day, every week the CEO's office receives at least one written or oral message from a delighted customer who simply says — and I paraphrase — what a pleasure it is to get a human being within three rings, and a human being who knows what she or he is talking about!

There are no shortcuts in sports; likewise, there are no shortcuts in business. One needs to know when a sixty to eighty-hour week is necessary and when a forty-hour week will do the job. What about during crunch times? It is okay to expect employees to work more than a forty-hour week at strategic times provided you explain the brutal facts and all the issues to them so they know why their efforts are essential. If it is short-term and employees are strategically engaged, it can actually increase employee trust in senior management. We get good feedback through our employee climate surveys, which tell us that the employees are more than willing to put in the extra time — fifty or sixty hour work weeks — if they understand the game plan that we have communicated clearly and honestly with them. In fact, some of the highest scores we ever achieved on climate surveys were the years where the expectations were the highest and employees were required to work longer hours. In reflecting upon that, three things come to mind:

- Employees are proud to be a part of a strategic initiative to which they contribute.

- We were up front in the beginning that everyone, from top to bottom, needed to put in the extra hours.

- Because of 1 and 2, employees understood this would be good for their careers, create future opportunities and keep NEDD vital.

A lifelong pursuit of professional and personal development — playing all out to be the best you can be — will enhance your life immeasurably and will also benefit all those whose lives you impact. If no one else is "raising the bar" and encouraging you to grow and develop in new and more challenging ways, it is up to you to raise the bar yourself. Let me give you a personal example from my own life. NEDD is the major sponsor of the Mount Washington Road Race, one of the most challenging mountain courses in the country. I have run it three times, and I have worked hard to improve my race times since I started running ten years ago. I took the same approach that I use in the office and put in the work, running many more miles per week than I might have wanted to. This hard work translated to my 5k running times going from twenty-five minutes to twenty-one minutes. Those of you who run and are over age fifty recognize that to improve four minutes at a 5k distance is not an easy thing, but again, it is all about putting in the work. In the course of studying great runners and understanding the sport so I could improve, I learned that outstanding running requires four attributes:

• Putting in the miles (putting in the work!)

• Having natural talent

• Keeping a balance between putting in the work and staying injury-free

• Knowing how much pain you want to put up with in a race

Of these four attributes, putting in the work is the most important according to runners, from elite to recreational, with whom I have spoken.

Playing all out means continuing our personal and professional development. Continuing — throughout our lives — our personal and professional development not only helps us to prepare for new work possibilities, it makes us interesting people to be around, keeps us passionate about life, and benefits those whose lives we influence. Our lives are richer, and our interests and skills more well rounded. If you want to be a well-rounded leader, you will find ways to lead both in your workplace and in your community. "Everybody cannot be famous. But everybody can be great, because greatness is determined by service," Dr. Martin Luther King, Jr. said.

When Steve Forbes visited New Hampshire a few years ago, he challenged us: "You've got to get through this short-term turbulence, but you also have to ask, if you desire to grow, where do you want to be five years from now and what do you have to do to put yourself in a position, when the economy grows again as it will, to be able to take advantage of it?" He was referring to financial investment strategies, but I would like us to apply those thoughts to the investments we make in ourselves and in others.

Investing in your education, relationships and leadership potential are three fundamental facets of investing in your work life. Max Dupree says this about work: "Work should be, and can be, productive and rewarding, meaningful and maturing, enriching and fulfilling, healing and joyful. Work is one of our greatest privileges."

THE BIG RED FACTOR

Outwork the average person and be a role model for your teammates. This creates the environment where people will admire you as a leader and where the company will flourish with you as a role model. H. L. Mencken once said, "For every complex problem, there is an answer that is clear, simple and wrong." However, I do have one simple answer to offer that I have heard from all successful business people and athletes: play all out and put in the work. If you do, you can't go wrong. Dr. Pearl Kane, from Columbia University, at a speech at the Holderness School graduation in 2010, made a point that resonates strongly with me. Her theme was that one's success and impact are directly proportional to one's efforts, hard work and in connecting with people, and not necessarily one's natural intelligence. We can't control our natural intelligence, but all of us can work hard, like Big Red.

Chapter 5

Earn Trust

*"What you are as a person is far more important
than what you are as a basketball player."*

– John Wooden

*When I walked out onto the basketball court to practice, scrimmage
or play a regular season game, I had total trust in my teammates that they
would put forth an unfailing effort and make all their decisions in the best
interest of the team, attempting to do the right thing at the right time for
the right reason.*

– Dave Cowens

The famous football coach of the New England Patriots, Bill Belichick,
is one of the top seven professional football coaches of all time, according
to a 2013 ESPN study. Coach Belichick often says in interviews that the
key to success is trusting teammates, with everyone doing his job the way
he should.

In every successful company, every job is an important job; it is just that each job is different. For example, I know I can trust my colleagues in the mailroom at Northeast Delta Dental (NEDD) to demonstrate exemplary customer service by sending out explanation of benefits notifications to customers and checks to dentists within the timeframe that we have guaranteed them. Without the effort of this team in the mailroom, Northeast Delta Dental would not be as successful.

This trust in your teammates is a critical success factor. If your relationship with your coworkers is not trusting, if you feel you are being second-guessed, or if a person or department does not live up to company standards, the result is detrimental to the long-term success of the company. We all have to be trusted in order to do our best work. Board members and top leaders have to be free to concentrate on strategic plans, policy, the competition and vision. The employees responsible for the day-to-day work have to trust their managers if they are going to be as productive as possible.

We strive to create a culture where employees can be the best they can be and where trust is nurtured, whether it is with the employees, our three Boards of Directors and Trustees, our customers, our participating member dentists, or any other stakeholders, such as our regulators at the Department of Insurance and our political leaders. A total trust company has low stress and tension at work, which results in less absenteeism and turnover.

When asked what activities, programs and other experiences have had the most significant impact on NEDD's progress as an organization, I answer it is trust. All activities, all communication, all growth — among employees and between employees and customers — are a lot quicker and easier when you are a total trust company. Stephen M. R. Covey calls this the "Speed of Trust." Trust speeds up work and builds a solid team. Covey maintains that trust is more important than vision, strategy, systems, infrastructure and skills, and he concludes that "leading at the speed of trust is both financially rewarding and just plain fun and energizing." NEDD's employees couldn't agree more! Here is a summary of Covey's behaviors of high trust leaders, with a sprinkling of Jim Collins. They are:

1. Keep commitments. (I think this is the most important at NEDD, where we always try to under-promise and over-deliver.)
2. Demonstrate respect.
3. Create transparency.
4. Right wrongs.
5. Show loyalty.
6. Deliver results.
7. Get better.
8. Confront reality. (This is what Collins calls "Confront the Brutal Facts".)
9. Clarify expectations.
10. Practice accountability.
11. Listen first.
12. Talk straight. (Say what you mean and mean what you say.)
13. Extend trust.

How do we build trust? First, be consistent in your behaviors, in and outside the boardroom. Next, consistently do the right thing even when no one is watching. This develops trust among employees as well as between the company and its customers, gracefully guiding the organization to sustainable success.

Let's start with consistency. Hard as it may be, we leaders have to remember to stick to our guns when it comes to how we lead. Avoid a "flavor of the month" leadership style. Business consultant Cliff Moore taught me this: a leader loses credibility by introducing a concept and then going on to the next hot topic in business a short while later. If we do this, employees soon realize that if they just hang in there, this new business philosophy shall pass and they can go back to status quo. I recall at John Hancock Insurance Company in Boston (my first employer), being introduced to the latest business tool by executives in three-piece suits (we called these guys "the suits"), who soon went on to a new department and the latest business fad. As young employees, we learned to pay the suits and their concepts lip service. I remembered this twenty years later at NEDD, when I was introducing all our employees to our

Guarantee Of Service Excellence^SM program (*described in* **Chapter 9**) and our commitment to excellence in all aspects of our work. I explained to all NEDD employees that the guarantee and excellence were part of my ten-year plan, I was here at NEDD for the long run and that we could accomplish great things at NEDD if we stayed the course. Sure enough, one year later, in 1996, Northeast Delta Dental, once a lesser-known company in New Hampshire, was featured in New Hampshire's two largest newspapers, the *Union Leader* and the *Concord Monitor*.

Two of Northeast Delta Dental's core values are teamwork (working effectively toward a shared mission) and integrity (being respectfully honest and responsive to internal and external customers). As part of the way we live those values, everyone on the leadership team encourages employees to feel genuinely empowered to achieve our mission, which includes making decisions that will delight our customers. We know that all of us on the leadership team must walk the talk if we are going to earn and grow trust. What happens if we say we are all working toward our common mission and believe in respectful empowerment but do not listen to employee suggestions? What if we do not reward employees who try to delight the customers when their actions differ from what we would have done ourselves? Then we are likely to build a culture of fear or insecurity rather than a culture of trust. Each time we have a choice of living our values or not, we face what Scandinavian Airlines' former leader and CEO, Jan Carlzon, used to call a "Moment of Truth." If our actions as leaders consistently embody our values of teamwork and integrity, we will build trust. If we are inconsistent (or worse, if we consistently ignore our values), we will appear untrustworthy at best.

One example of the way we empower our employees is that NEDD's customer service representatives are empowered to make exceptions on the fly over the telephone on dental claim payments if, in their opinion, it's warranted. Our customer service representatives understand they must demonstrate integrity in these situations. I am confident that they do, so much so that neither a vice president nor I must sign off on a claim payment exception processed by a customer service representative.

As trust grows, the cost of the transaction decreases, and the speed of the transaction increases. Our largest real estate and construction project, which was our new headquarters in Concord, New Hampshire, was built by Hutter Construction. Because we had learned to trust each other, we began this work simply on a handshake.

Integrity is another of NEDD's important corporate values. I try to be a role model for others when it comes to integrity. Peter Northouse in his seminal book *Leadership: Theory and Practice* defines integrity as follows: "Integrity is the quality of honesty and trustworthiness. People who adhere to a strong set of principles and take responsibility for their actions are exhibiting integrity. Leaders with integrity inspire confidence in others because they can be trusted to do what they say they are going to do. They are loyal, dependable and not deceptive. Basically, integrity makes a leader believable and worthy of trust."

I try to act with integrity in all I do because then I can demand it of everyone else on my team. At times, this has proven very challenging, and it has not been clear how to act with the greatest integrity. I would like to describe a time when my own integrity and that of NEDD was on the line and how I dealt with it. First, a little background.

NEDD is actually composed of three separate legal entities (serving Maine, New Hampshire and Vermont). One of these entities, Delta Dental Plan of New Hampshire (DDPNH) was originally formed by an act of the state legislature in 1961 with great support from New Hampshire dentists. Early on, DDPNH participation rules required dentists to give back a percentage of every dental claim payment made to them in order to establish proper insurance reserves. This created a "psychological" ownership of DDPNH by dentists in the community, and the by-laws of the corporation enabled participating dentists (that is, those dentists who signed contractual agreements with Northeast Delta Dental) to vote on who serves on the DDPNH Board of Directors.

This governance system worked well until about the time they hired me as CEO in 1995. Nine of the fifteen members of the DDPNH Board of Directors who hired me were voted off the Board within eighteen months of my arrival (having nothing to do with me). This occurred because these DDPNH Board Members, in the best interests of the corporation, attempted to add two new products — managed care and preferred provider products — to our product line to meet changing needs in the

46

marketplace. Some dentists felt these new products would lower our payments to them and hurt their bottom line. This was debatable, but many dentists felt it to be true.

So here was my integrity test: to prevent this turmoil and disruptive turnover caused by the constant "dis-election" of DDPNH Board members, the legislature decided to act. They did this at the urging of our major customers, founding fathers, and concerned citizens who all wanted the by-laws of the corporation changed so that the dentists could no longer elect the DDPNH Board of Directors. A legislative bill (Senate Bill 308) was drafted, and I would have to explain my position and to testify on this bill. Members of the existing Board of Directors — two of whom resigned over this — wanted to keep the status quo and were not in favor of SB308. Many of our other stakeholders and customers wanted me to lobby in favor of changing the corporate governance. I knew, in my heart and in my head, the status quo was not in the best interest of the long-term health of the corporation. What was I to do? Everyone was watching me to see which side I would come down on, and the legislature expected me to take the lead. To top it off, several of our dentists filed a lawsuit against DDPNH, claiming that a past Board decision having to do with managed care was illegal.

Barbara McLaughlin, Director of Corporate Relations and my most trusted colleague, and I spent long days and weeks thinking about the right action to take. Where did the path of integrity lie? I owed a duty of loyalty to my current Board or bosses as well as to the customers and the corporation on a long-term basis.

This brainstorming led us to leverage the fact that DDPNH was not "owned" by the member dentists but by the citizens of New Hampshire because we were legally incorporated as a 501(c)(4) charitable trust. We realized we should emphasize that NEDD served three primary kinds of stakeholders (dentists, the group purchasers who bought our insurance products, and the individuals or subscribers covered by our insurance), and that our duty was to balance the interests of all these stakeholders if we were to fulfill our mission. Our research revealed that other Delta Dental plans were often incorporated under very different statutes or follow very different by-laws. Even at our own Delta Dental Plan of

Maine, the individuals covered by their insurance were considered the members of the corporation.

The approach I took was to respond factually to questions posed by the legislators, talk about governance best practices (a topic on which I have expertise and experience), and describe how other Delta Dental corporations were governed. Because I took this fact-based approach, I was ethically able to present

...consistently do the right thing even when no one is watching.

a well-considered response to our Board members, customers, dentists, the public and the legislature. When the press quoted me concerning the proposed Senate Bill 308, nobody could figure out, in a good way, which side I was on. I was just presenting the facts.

The result was that the New Hampshire legislature developed a good governance model for DDPNH that assured the future success of the corporation while retaining the helpful input of our participating dentists. It still required seven seats for dentists on the DDPNH Board of fifteen members. But now the dentists could no longer vote in their friends or vote out those with whom they disagreed. The other eight members of the DDPNH Board consist of four non-dentist individual consumers or public members, and four professionals who are purchasers of our insurance. They are usually human resource and other professionals who do the benefits decision-making in their corporation and are experts in the field. That means that the DDPNH Board has a balance of dentists, individual insurance customers and group insurance purchasers. All fifteen DDPNH Board members are now vetted, evaluated, interviewed and recommended for election by an External Nominating Committee.

It works! DDPNH now stands as a model of excellence in corporate governance, and other companies often use us as a benchmark for our best governance practices. (We also won a summary judgment on the lawsuit filed by the dentists.)

The Solomaic approach taken by the legislators and me to the new governance of the corporation was in no small way the determining factor in the continuing success of the company. Without the governance enacted by SB308, the necessary new PPO and direct to consumer products would not be possible, and the company's future would now be at risk. Moreover, without this approach, we would not have been able to avoid casualties as we did. That is, we lost no customers and no participating dentists, and I retained my job!

As CEO, with Barbara's help, I had to harness resources and points of view on both sides of the issue. I had to consider the best interests of all our stakeholders, and I had to be strictly honest, balanced and factual in my testimony and behavior. It was not easy to know what to do, but I believe I took the path of greatest integrity and it led to the best possible results.

You must tell the truth when forming solid working relationships because that is the only way to establish trust in one another. Managers need to tell employees what they expect of them. They should then encourage employees to ask questions concerning these job requirements. Fellow workers need to work in an environment that encourages sharing their opinions and working towards a common goal outlined by their superiors.

Now, if you act on the NEDD values, everyone can disagree with a decision if things don't go according to plan, but they can never question your motives. To do this breeds discontent and a lack of harmony. In a public arena, it is always paramount to display respect for your teammates and managers, and this must be a two-way street. Tone is set at the top. The leadership team sets the tone by example and by consistent behaviors, forming the culture of the organization, business or sports franchise.

As Dave might say, when there is disagreement or strife within the team, it must be hammered out in the confines of the locker room (or in NEDD's case the boardroom) and kept in confidence. Just think what it would be like if all of your workday phone calls and meetings were on public display. What if millions of people were watching your every move and people were wagering money on your daily performance? My guess is that no one in the company would risk embarrassing others or act in a disrespectful manner. If they did, what a can of worms that would open up, and what a distraction that would be. My co-author, Barbara McLaughlin, set an excellent example: she always held the meeting details of our NEDD Boards of Directors and financial information close to the vest, never once breaching the highest level of confidentiality.

Internal trust leads to external trust. If there is trust among your employees, that will shine through to your external customers who also trust your organization. External customers who trust the company will give you the benefit of a doubt when a mistake happens. We are all human, and even the best companies and most highly empowered service representatives make mistakes. Those external customers will stick with you, and you will not feel the financial impact on your bottom line that you would have felt without trust. Quality guru Christopher Hart often says that a total trust company grows its business because the external customer has complete confidence in the company.

Because Northeast Delta Dental's customers have learned to trust us, even when we make a mistake, they give us the benefit of the doubt as we work to correct the error and prevent it from reoccurring. This means that our reputation does not suffer in the same way that it would if we made the same mistake but had not earned our customers' trust.

NEDD's customers know we have a long and consistent history of delivering quality service, and we will do immediate service recovery. Our customers have seen that NEDD will genuinely acknowledge its mistakes, often turning ourselves in via our written Guarantee Of Service Excellence^{SM}, which promises customers that they can expect certain high levels of performance from us. *(Please see **Chapter 9: Please Your Fans** for details of this service guarantee and its impact.)* We admit our mistakes with sincerity, coupled with an explanation of what NEDD plans to do to prevent the mistake from happening again.

We conduct a formal employee satisfaction assessment survey every other year. Because we care so much about trust, we have also built and use other listening posts that are easily available to the leadership team. These include interviews with employees after their first three months on the job, our trademark Coffee with the Coach get-togethers coordinated by the human resources team, and a candid review and audit of exit interviews when employees leave for new outside opportunities.

When any employee leaves Northeast Delta Dental, we often celebrate it as a promotion outside of the company, and we are happy for the individual. It is also an opportunity for us to learn whether s/he left because of a flaw in the organization.

I like to say at our All Colleagues Meetings that everyone's job is as important as everyone else's, that while each of our positions is different, each is equally valuable. I would like to thank Aaron Spencer, Founder and Chairman Emeritus of Uno Chicago Grill, with whom I served on a human resources panel in the spring of 2011, for codifying that thought. With his help I have learned that, when employees are treated fairly as valued members of a team, when they understand the game plan and the business and corporate strategy, they do their jobs better. Their understanding and trust in the organization gives them more depth of knowledge of what they do and why they do it, which in turn grows the company. When we show we trust our employees, they will trust us and perform at their best. Without trust, respect and fairness, an organization requires many rules of conduct, and this is not a good way to operate. In contrast, when people know the right thing to do and can be trusted to do it without management oversight, the entire organization operates at its best.

Building trust is a fine art, not an exact science. The best way to build a culture of trust (in accordance with the core values of teamwork and integrity) is definitely NOT to try to create a recipe book or set of written policies and procedures that aim to cover all possible situations. Instead, the best way to build a culture of trust is for all leaders or coaches to be honest and consistent in their actions and to show trust in the employees or players by empowering them, by trusting them, to contribute to the organization's mission to the best of their abilities. This will build their confidence and increases their ability to please customers.

I have found that trusting in my organization's ability to do good and do well by focusing on people first frees me up to be and give my best.

THE BIG RED FACTOR

The success of a sports franchise or a business relates to the organization's ability to promote genuine trust up and down the organization, between employee teammates and the CEO and other top leaders (just as between players and a coach).

An atmosphere of trust between management and employees in which each assumes the other will do the right thing and, to the greatest extent possible, act in each other's respective best interests, frees everyone to act in the best interests of the team. Managers treat employees consistently: management's walk (behavior) matches management's talk (statements).

Second Quarter

"He who believes in nobody knows that he himself is not to be trusted."

– Red Auerbach

Chapter 6

Play as a Team

"My responsibility is getting all my players playing for the name on the front of the jersey, not the one on the back."

— Unknown

My very first day of training camp at Hellenic College in Brookline Mass, a Greek orthodox seminary, I had an idea. JoJo White was the Celtics veteran point guard and one of its better players. In basketball, every player works harmoniously with all the others but the point guard and center have to have a closer relationship than with others. I decided that I would seek JoJo out and offer to rebound for him whenever he wanted to work on his perimeter shooting, and I did. This single act of being willing to do something for another person with no strings attached set a tone. He didn't know me and I didn't know him, but I know he appreciated the fact that I offered to help him work on his game.

By doing this, I was making myself aware of how his shots rebounded and the timing of his release. Each player has certain nuances to his shot.

Some shoot in a flat line. Some arc the ball. Also, I was working on my rebound conditioning and timing. In the back of my mind I knew that if he knew I was totally in his corner he would be very willing to pass me the ball when I was open. So the beginning of our relationship was a positive one. You know what they say about only getting one chance to make a first impression. This positive feedback was freely given within our team, among teammates. We had a very unselfish unit, knew our strengths and weaknesses, and worked well together to accomplish the goal of everyone trying to do the right thing at the right time for the right reason.

– Dave Cowens

In work, as in sports, there is room for people who are bridge builders. To the extent that they enable us to work together cooperatively rather than competitively, the bridges we build with each other will be securely anchored, will have strong support systems, and will help us all win — just as Dave did by building a bridge with JoJo. Businesses, like teams, need employees and players who can work together cooperatively and who are not afraid to make their colleagues look good. No matter how great individual players are, the team will do better when the players cooperate and play as a team. That means playing selflessly — thinking about the team score instead of individual statistics.

Do you have a quiet captain in your organization that leads by example? Someone who can be the ambassador of consistent exemplary performance? Someone who lives your corporate values — such as accountability — and does this in a humble way such as John Havlicek? Remember, John Havlicek was a leader among leaders because five members of the 1974 Celtics championship team later became NBA coaches. That's Don Chaney, Don Nelson (the man with the most coaching wins in NBA history), Paul Silas, Paul Westphal and Dave "Big Red" Cowens himself.

I have found the best way to cascade our corporate values is by way of informal team captains, à la John Havlicek, who quietly lead by example and model the behavior you would like others to follow. Now, when it comes to risk taking and empowerment, Northeast Delta Dental (NEDD), like every role model company with which I am familiar, trains employees so they are prepared to make frontline customer service decisions based on their area of expertise and the best information.

This is why it is so important to the value of the franchise to employ a star player. You need someone who becomes the bedrock of your team in the arena. This must be a person of great character who maintains a very high degree of sports ethics and is unselfish, stays highly prepared, advocates unequivocally the coach's philosophy, has humility, respect for the game being played, and is the best player on the team by performing (especially at crunch time) like the best player on the team. The star player, in essence, is someone you can always count on to try to do the right thing, at the right time, for the right reason.

Teamwork doesn't just happen. Coaches and CEOs have to build it consciously. Coaches and CEOs have to let the players make some of the decisions during a game. In business, we call that empowerment — when employees who are closest to the action get to make decisions for the good of the organization.

Employee empowerment is an important but much-overused phrase in corporate America. It got early traction when managers noticed the success of certain Japanese companies that empowered employees to work in teams. For example, some Japanese car companies built cars in a team approach: a whole team building one car, as contrasted with each employee doing one mundane function on an assembly line all day for many cars. This allowed workers to learn and do more than one task and to share responsibilities as they felt best.

The Malcolm Baldrige National Quality Award Criteria emphasizes empowerment. These criteria point out that organizations benefit when they actively take advantage of the innovative wisdom of their employees. In my opinion, The Baldrige Award, established in the late 1980s, was the first comprehensive and integrated description of all the principles of successful organizations. Although the criteria have matured over the past twenty-five or so years, the principles have stood the test of time.

Organizations that use these fundamental principles — such as empowerment, visionary leadership, organizational and personal learning, valuing the workforce, customer-focused excellence, managing by fact, social responsibility and continuous learning — have been proven to out-perform organizations in the same market that do not adhere to the principles. I strongly recommend that all current or future leaders obtain and study a copy of the *Baldrige Criteria for Performance Excellence*. I have used Baldrige principles from the beginning, and I find them invaluable.

Empowerment also underlies the switch from Theory X management style to Theory Y management style. Theory X, as most people know, is when management controls everything and assumes employees don't know much. Theory Y, on the other hand, assumes the frontline employees are in the best possible position to understand their jobs and do what is best for customers. Their managers believe employees are intelligent and will make the right decisions. Both Theory X and Y are well documented in Douglas McGregor's book, *The Human Side of Enterprise*.

A famous *Harvard Business Review* article, "Beyond Theory Y," establishes the notion that management needs to be situational, i.e., there may be times when Theory Y is appropriate, but there also may be times when Theory X could be more appropriate. For example, in the middle of a massive systems conversion, experienced managers may need to be nimble and be able to make quick informed decisions without much employee input. When I was leading the start-up of Delta Dental of Massachusetts, we had only nine months to hire 100 people and set up systems and a claim office/customer service facility. There were times, no doubt, when I tracked more closely with Theory X management principles in the interest of making firm deadlines, without which Delta Dental of Massachusetts would have been at risk. This was especially true because Blue Cross Blue Shield of Massachusetts was ready to pounce on any corporate weakness of Delta Dental of Massachusetts.

At other times, input from employees leads to wiser decision-making. When designing new products, Theory Y is probably the better way to go. This is all situational leadership. As described by Peter G. Northouse in *Leadership: Theory and Practice*, situational leadership "...stresses that leadership is composed of both a directive and supportive dimension, and that each has to be applied appropriately in a given situation. To determine what is needed in a particular situation, a leader must evaluate his or her employees and assess how competent and committed they are to perform a given task."

The 1990s built on situational leadership. Baldrige award-winning companies demonstrated their superiority in leadership, empowerment and financial and market results. Unfortunately, "employee empowerment" also became a marketing tool. President or Chair letters written for annual reports would espouse that "employees are our most important asset," and that the company "believes in empowerment." However, having done Baldrige-type examinations and visited many companies in my professional capacity, I often found that while they state they practice employee empowerment, an intensive examination and review of the actual corporate culture reveals that this simply is not so. Their employees tell you that, literally or by their actions.

True and genuine employee empowerment involves engaged and trained employees who understand the overarching strategy, who believe in the strategy and who have the appropriate education and tools to allow them to make the best decisions. I call these empowered employees "self-actualizing," using Abraham Maslow's term to mean they are achieving their full potential, expressing their creativity, and pursuing continuous learning and improvement. Truly empowered employees who have the tools and authority to make frontline decisions will enhance external customer service and delight the paying customer. Superb customer service, as business colleague Tom Manning once said to me, is "doing proactively with enthusiasm what you are going to eventually have to do when a customer demands it." Only an empowered workforce can implement and follow Tom Manning's ideal mantra.

At NEDD, one way we encourage empowerment and teamwork is through our extensive use of teams. We form teams to find solutions to workplace challenges and encourage team members to work together to find innovative solutions and solve problems so that everyone succeeds. The teams have charters outlining their purpose, and each team has a member of senior management assigned as a liaison who ensures the team gets needed resources and remains on track. Minutes from the team meetings are posted online, so they are accessible to all employees. Because the teams' progress is public and team members know they will be recognized for their contributions, the teams engender *esprit de corps*, collaborative approaches and success.

It is management's responsibility to make sure employees have the education or training to allow them to make appropriate decisions. When errors do occur, we celebrate the mistake as a learning experience. Employees must understand in advance the parameters of their authority. This defines appropriate risk taking. For example, at Northeast Delta Dental, a frontline customer service representative can make a decision to pay a dental claim if the dental office provides the necessary information over the phone. S/he doesn't have to ask for an email trail, letter or fax. Of course, management at NEDD would not want a frontline customer service representative to approve a claim that's not oral health related, which would be outside our insurance license authority and would put the company at risk. Therefore, it is up to senior management to make sure the customer service representatives understand the dental insurance parameters,

At NEDD and other role model companies, each employee has a sense of ownership for an organization's success...

and that they are comfortable with their knowledge and empowerment. There can be a fine line between appropriate risk taking and approving something that could threaten our insurance license. A mistake in this area presents an opportunity for the employee to learn. Naturally, if an employee repeatedly makes the same mistake, a "learning moment" can ultimately become a performance issue for that employee's annual review.

Empowering individual employees or players is only part of creating good teams. It is also important to involve many employees or teammates in developing solutions to problems. While teams need to keep management in the loop, some of the best solutions come from teammates at the grassroots level. More often than not, it is the frontline employees, those closest to the action, who are in the best position to be problem-solvers and satisfy — or even delight — a customer.

One of the wonderful things about Dave Cowens and Larry Bird, two of my favorite Celtics (along with Bill Russell, Sam Jones, and John Havlicek), was that they were the ultimate team players and would do anything for the team, even if it meant their own personal statistics would suffer.

One marquee example is when Larry declined the rare opportunity for a quadruple double in a 1985 basketball game (double digits in points, rebounds, assists, and steals or blocked shots). This has only been done four times in the history of the NBA, and Larry had the opportunity, having completed a triple double with nine steals by the end of the third quarter. Larry had thirty points, twelve rebounds, ten assists, and nine steals for the Celtics when he was taken out in the third quarter of a game against the Utah Jazz, in a 110 to 94 victory for the Celtics. When informed of the rare individual opportunity to achieve the quadruple double, he declined. The game was in the bag, and there was no need for a personal accolade at the expense of the team. (What if Larry had gotten hurt in this pursuit of an individual accomplishment?)

In this day and age of ESPN and large multi-year contracts, how refreshing was it for us to witness Dave and Larry play at a championship level without worrying about their personal glorification. Ultimately, of course, Dave and Larry understood that the team's success would actually enhance their personal and professional success. Dave participated in two world championships, 1974 and 1976, and Larry won three rings in the 1980s. Other great basketball players such as Karl Malone, Charles Barkley and Patrick Ewing were among the top players of their time, but there is always a footnote that these three superstars never participated on a professional championship team.

At NEDD and other role model companies, each employee has a sense of ownership for an organization's success and the opportunity to contribute to the community at-large. That in turn provides the internal motivation to continue to do one's best for the success of the company team. "Ownership" can literally mean employee stock ownership in a public company, but at NEDD (where there are no stockholders), ownership means "buy in" and the feeling that "this is my company and I want it to succeed." We have educated our employees — and they believe it — that we have a responsibility to leave NEDD in a solid and thriving position for future citizens of Maine, New Hampshire, and Vermont.

When I meet with all of our employees at our All Colleagues Meetings, I often use the analogy that the most optimal employee is the Larry Bird or Dave Cowens of dental insurance. By that, I mean someone who is outstanding doing his or her own work (in Larry and Dave's case, both Hall of Famers) but also someone who makes his or her colleagues shine. This is important because human nature in a capitalist society is that individuals still want recognition for their individual contributions and want more compensation than employees who do less.

One of my most prized leadership books is Max DePree's *Leadership is an Art*. I value it beyond any other book on leadership I possess, and I recommend it more often than any other book in my library. DePree says, "Modern corporations should be communities, not battlefields. At their heart[s] lie covenants between executives and employees that rest on shared commitment to ideas, to issues, to values, to goals, and to management processes." He also says, "The condition of our hearts, the openness of our attitudes, the quality of our competence, the fidelity of our experience: these give vitality to the work experience and meaning to life."

What Max DePree is saying, in a much more philosophical way than I, is that teamwork and people are our most valuable assets. You cannot give that lip service and state it in an Annual Report without living it. Mr. DePree's book is also a seminal piece about servant leadership — the philosophy that the leader of the organization is in service to his or her employees, customers, and other stakeholders.

As CEO of NEDD, I aspire to the ideals and ideas of servant leadership. George Clements, Chairman of Jewel Tea Company, a national grocery chain, once said, "Work for those who work for you," and "Ninety percent of a leader's time should be doing *everything you can* to help your direct reports succeed. You should be the first assistant to the people who work for you." This is sometimes called "servant leadership" and is often viewed as contrarian or paradoxical because as Peter Northouse queries, "How can a person be a leader and a servant at the same time?" The answer, it seems to me based on my experience at NEDD, is that the employees, like team players, are even more inspired and will do even more for the organization, and go above and beyond, when they also see their coach or CEO putting the team ahead of personal ego. I have absorbed and followed the principles of servant leadership as first documented and coined by Robert Greenleaf in 1970, and summarized by Spears in 1998. These are:

- Listening

- Empathy

- Personal well being

- Awareness

- Persuasion

- Conceptualization

- Foresight

- Stewardship

- Commitment to the growth of people

- Building community

Following these principles helps foster a spirit of teamwork throughout NEDD.

Toastmasters International suggests another way of inspiring teamwork and cooperation. Some of you may be familiar with Toastmasters as an organization that builds presentation skills. Fewer people know it for its robust leadership-training track. Involvement in a Toastmasters club develops leadership skills as it builds communication skills, while it also offers valuable networking opportunities. A year's membership costs less than many presentation workshops, and the designations earned receive international recognition. Northeast Delta Dental chartered a community Toastmasters club ten years ago that we continue to host, and I have seen life-changing results in those who have participated. The Toastmasters International magazine identifies traits of effective leaders that I believe parallel the servant leadership list. These include:

- Making others feel important

- Promoting a vision

- Following the Golden Rule

- Admitting mistakes

- Criticizing others in private

- Staying close to the action

- Using the competitive drive correctly

THE BIG RED FACTOR

At the end of a game, fans remember the score for sure, but they also remember the character of the players they just watched. They remember whether the players worked as a team, whether they played all out, whether they played without ego and whether they gave it their all. When a team plays with teamwork, fans (like customers) remain loyal, and new fans notice and begin to attend. Companies, like sports teams, need to have employee ambassadors who are shining examples of shared company-wide values. Big Red, in the next chapter, describes how John Havlicek used to lead the Celtics to greatness in the 1970s in his humble, quiet way. Does your enterprise's corporate culture encourage the John Havlicek, Larry Bird and Dave Cowens

---

employees who are significant individual contributors but also make their colleagues shine? If you are in top management of your company, do you follow the tenets of servant leadership?

Chapter 7

Applaud Players Who Excel

*"What I do today is important because I am paying
a day of my life for it. What I accomplish must be
worthwhile because the price is high."* (Unknown)

– Barbara McLaughlin's life mantra

*In the 1970s, the Celtics won two championships (1974 and 1976)
and for most of that decade were an elite team in the National Basketball
Association. The acknowledged leader of our 1970's championship team
was our captain, John Havlicek. John never spoke about it, but all of the
players on our team — the stars such as JoJo White and all the veteran
players who went on to be head coaches in the NBA — acknowledged
John as our leader because he always conducted himself as the ultimate
professional. He was a clutch performer everyone could always count on
to do the right thing at the right time and for the right reason.*

*I have received far too much acclaim over the last forty years of my
life for doing something that was very exciting and stimulating for me.*

But the lasting and most cherished rewards that I receive are just simple compliments from people who enjoyed watching me play basketball.

– Dave Cowens

In the previous chapter, I talked a lot about empowerment and teamwork. The complement to empowerment is, of course, accountability. In all the best companies I have seen, including my own, each employee is accountable for his or her own actions, reinforced by the quiet captains, referenced by Dave, who model the behaviors and values, such as accountability, that propel the organization to greatness.

As Dave mentions, good coaches also have to think about how to recognize and reward their players who excel. For Dave, as for many employees, the recognition or a simple compliment is important. For others, a monetary reward is also appreciated. This chapter covers all three issues — accountability, recognition, and rewards — as part of the system of applauding players or employees who excel.

At Northeast Delta Dental (NEDD), we do a lot of storytelling to illustrate our values and goals. Remember the famous Federal Express anecdote of an employee renting a helicopter to get a package to the top of a mountainside? Many years ago, to stoke the flames of empowerment, I would say to my employees, "Feel free to rent a helicopter" to get a claim paid. Of course, dental plans have maximum controls, so this is not as big a leap of faith as renting a helicopter, but I worked to ingrain the idea that I expected employees to take all appropriate measures to satisfy and even delight a customer.

On the other hand, if a customer service representative approved a claim outside our insurance guidelines, that employee would be accountable for that strategic error. The key is finding that balance between empowerment and accountability. Senior management needs to provide guidance by practice and by example, which is why we showcased "renting helicopters" at All Colleagues Meetings.

There are many ways NEDD documents and reviews accountability. On the one hand, we do not have a lot of policies and recipes. We expect employees to do the right thing, defined as following our core values of integrity, open communication, teamwork and quality. We do, however, have formal twice-yearly performance reviews. Supervisors evaluate how employees adhere to our value system, examine their use of empowerment and review their work.

Almost every week I receive a voicemail, email or note from a happy customer or dental office team member. We share these at All Colleagues Meetings or in our *Team Power* internal newsletter. All customers or dentists providing us with this feedback "gift" (and it is a gift to us) receive a letter from me, thanking them for their feedback, with a copy to the customer service representative who provided the great service. This, of course, positively reinforces the behavior we wish our customer service representatives to emulate and for which we hold them accountable.

Because there is an expectation of open communication (which I will review in the next chapter) and continuous feedback, when we do our formal performance review process, there is never a surprise between the manager and employee. In one respect, the review is simply a codification and documentation of what the manager and employee already know.

For example, we keep track of outstanding customer service by completely documenting feedback in what we call a "Me File." These are anecdotal acknowledgements from our dentists and customers, both internal and external, praising the outstanding performance of employees. Every employee at NEDD, from the CEO to the mailroom, keeps a "Me File." I incorporate my notes in a portfolio reviewed by the Board's Compensation Committee. For others at NEDD, much of this praise reaches my office, giving me the opportunity to recognize the employee and customer involved robustly.

If there are performance issues or concerns during the year or if there is a service failure directly related to an employee's performance, the manager also documents this information in the performance review. However, as a learning and development company, we take the approach that a mistake is a learning opportunity or a teaching moment. While we hold an employee accountable, learning from mistakes will ultimately improve the performance of the corporation as a whole.

Another example of accountability is our exit interviews, both with departing employees and with our Board members who leave when their term limits expire. These formal processes work where employees and Board members can "tell it like it is" and are assured of confidentiality. Of course, if the individual wants that information to be shared in the spirit of continuous improvement, then that information will certainly be shared with the goal of improving the corporation. Our Corporate Board Chairs and the Chairs of the Governance Committees have an opportunity to review all exit interviews and performance reviews of our senior management team and Board member exit interviews.

Accountability would mean little without recognition. When employees are accountable for and excel in their performance, our first action is to recognize or applaud this excellence. Our goal is to acknowledge the employee's contribution and recognize the accomplishments in consistent and meaningful ways. Showing appreciation is an important component of creating a positive culture. We do this recognition in many ways.

I have already mentioned the letters of thanks from customers that we share and document. Another example of the way NEDD recognizes employees is TEAM Grams. TEAM is an acronym for Together Everyone Achieves More. These are short notes from one employee to another completed on an ad-hoc basis. They are a simple thank you from one employee to another for their contribution that resulted in achievement of a deliverable to either an internal or an external customer. We post these on-line on our intranet and publish them in our monthly employee newsletter, *Team Power*.

I have found that notes to employees from me, recognizing a birthday or key anniversary and offering simple gratitude, positively reinforce a supportive culture more than any monetary award can. This is a surprisingly motivating tool. Each employee receives a birthday card with a $50 check. More importantly, I sign each card individually and include a special note.

NEDD also recognizes corporate anniversaries in a multitude of ways. Significant anniversaries (five years, ten years, up to forty years and climbing longevity) receive a coveted gold lapel pin of the Delta logo embedded with a precious stone indicating their years of service. We also engrave their names on recognition plaques prominently displayed on our campus at both of our buildings at One and Two Delta Drive. Employees achieving twenty-five years with Northeast Delta Dental are inducted into our Quarter Century Club and are recognized on a special plaque designed specifically for that significant achievement. We display this, too, prominently on our campus at both building locations. Additionally, the individual employee receives a personalized handsome plaque to display in his or her workspace. Beyond these milestone dates, we note every anniversary, from one year onward, at the beginning of every quarterly All Colleagues Meeting. Finally, employees who have retired or who have passed away have their names and significant milestones recognized on plaques displayed at both locations.

The combination of recognizing experienced employees whose longevity is highly valued as well as the one-year anniversaries of newer employees has proven to be a great recipe for success. New employees value the wisdom and institutional knowledge of veteran employees; in turn, seasoned employees value the new perspective and ideas of emerging employees. Significantly, the company values both!

The senior management team, which meets regularly, also dedicates time each week signing cards for employees commemorating moments in life. These may range from get-well cards or sympathy cards on the loss of family members, to celebrations in life such as marriage or the birth of a baby, and more. As CEO, I also send a special baby book and note to employees who become moms or dads for the first time. NEDD has also found that surprise rewards are highly motivating — this can range from an on-the-spot unexpected bonus for a job well done to a more significant one-time bonus for a milestone accomplishment. NEDD employees are also motivated by our holding special events involving nutritional food, such as our annual mid-summer employee appreciation cookout (sometimes spouses are included — we let employees decide), as well as ice cream socials and special breakfast and luncheon events that raise money for our signature Helping Hands program.

We have learned over time that people love to see and hear their name displayed or spoken aloud at All Colleagues Meetings, luncheons, our summer party, and at our annual holiday party, held every December. They love to see their name in print in our massive year-end board report, which highlights all of the great works our employees do throughout the year. Unlike many companies that have done away with holiday parties, we believe ours is a meaningful tradition that makes a difference. We have a history of such traditions.

As I said earlier, I like to call the most optimal NEDD employee the Larry Bird or Dave Cowens of Northeast Delta Dental, i.e., a superior individual who also makes his or her teammates shine. When NEDD had its acclaimed Far Exceeds employee recognition program, the criteria specified that not only must the individuals excel in their primary positions, but they must also effectively work on teams to let their brilliance shine on fellow employees. Three people have achieved Far Exceeds status each year for ten years in a row, earning Hall of Fame status. They are Barbara McLaughlin, Debbye Tardiff and Debbie LaValley.

We reward employees in monetary as well as non-monetary ways for their contributions and accomplishments. We have an annual special bonus recognizing employees' longevity with the company. Significantly, employees tell me that the most motivating of the recognitions are the non-monetary methods, especially hand-written notes from the CEO. That is not to say that monetary rewards are not important. We understand that without money there is no oral health mission. Similarly, employees need to take care of themselves and their families, which, in the final analysis, requires money. So, while I'll be first to say simple non-monetary accolades are motivational and inspirational, a company should also have team and individual monetary rewards to recognize employees for group, organizational, and individual accomplishments.

At NEDD, we have blended the human need for rewards for individual skills with contributions as a team member. Everyone in the company, from the CEO on down, receives a team bonus based on four key balanced scorecard metrics: Financial Perspective, Customer Perspective, Internal Perspective, and Innovation Learning and Growth Perspective. Within each of these metrics are objectives and measures to which everyone in the company contributes.

We have a significant balanced scorecard and S.M.A.R.T. goal process (S.M.A.R.T. = specific, measurable, attainable, relevant, timely), both of which are designed to recognize the accomplishments of the corporation and recognize individual and divisional superior contributions. *(Please see Chapter 10: Pay Attention to the Score.)*

This "teamshare" approach, using a balanced scorecard and now S.M.A.R.T. goals, encourages everyone in the corporation to row in the same direction and to realize that they can make important contributions to the success of the company. Nevertheless, we recognize that some employees are like Dave and Larry, MVP types, while some employees are less productive but still important. Therefore, in addition to the teamshare bonus, we evaluate each employee on his or her individual contribution. We review individuals semi-annually and annually, while we report the company achievements to everyone monthly so everyone knows where we stand. When we have high achievement and meet all our company goals, our Boards of Directors or Trustees approve a monetary reward.

> This "teamshare" approach... encourages everyone in the corporation to realize that they can make important contributions to the success of the company.

We reinforce teamwork and incentives for teamwork via carefully planned human resource training programs that encourage managers, directors and vice presidents to be like coaches and mentors, who want their direct employees to shine. They want to provide all the opportunities available for their employees to learn and develop new skills and progress and advance within NEDD.

THE BIG RED FACTOR

There is not a player around who doesn't appreciate applause for a great performance. Employees are no different. They need to know what is expected of them and for what they are accountable. Then, if they do well, they want to be recognized and rewarded. At NEDD, just as for professional athletes, we base the monetary rewards on team performance as well as individual performance. Nevertheless, many believe that personal recognition, such as

---

being named an MVP or acknowledged as a clutch player, is often more important to a person's well being than a bonus. As Abraham Maslow said in his 1943 paper "A Theory of Human Motivation," if our basic needs are met, we can be motivated by higher values to higher performance. Players and employees who are not worried about their physical well being or safety (Maslow's basic levels in his hierarchy of needs) will focus on delivering superior performance when they are motivated and inspired by a sense of belonging to a group they care about and by knowing they are esteemed. That is why accountability followed by fair and prompt recognition and rewards can be so effective. We all need to applaud all our players who excel.

Third Quarter

"Success is peace of mind, which is a direct result of self-satisfaction in knowing you did your best to become the best you are capable of becoming."

– John Wooden

Chapter 8

Communicate to Win

"Communication does not always occur naturally, even among a tight-knit group of individuals. Communication must be taught and practiced in order to bring everyone together as one."

– Mike Krzyzewski

I've never played a game where open communication wasn't an integral part of the action. From the coach defining our game plan, to each player shouting commands to each other throughout the contest, open communication is essential in getting the job done well.

In sports, the coach makes the final decisions on which plays to run at specific times during the game. The players have the responsibility to execute the called play but have the freedom to run something else if the opposing team does something that makes it impossible to follow the original plan. The trust the coach has in his players by instilling freedom in them to make the proper decisions is fueled by open communication. It's important to note that not all players are equally qualified to make these types of in-game decisions. One has to earn that right through trial and error. Most often, the players who make good things happen are the ones who everyone looks to as the leaders and are the ones we listen to.

In my rookie year with the Celtics, at six-foot-nine-inches, playing against seven-foot-two Kareem Abdul-Jabbar was a challenge. Kareem would pick his spot on the floor, and could score at will. Working together, my Celtics teammates and I developed a defense that would lessen Kareem's dominance and help move Kareem away from his favorite spot on the floor; otherwise, his dominance would have him scoring forty points against my thirty points. I, of course, kept Coach Tommy Heinsohn in the communication loop, but it was really the players who solved the problem.

Many fans tell me that when they watch a game it looks as though the players are not running plays but just freelancing all the time. This is the furthest thing from the truth. Most of the action in all sports is scripted. In other words, the players are working in harmony together. They're putting all the practice time spent working on all the various situations that can happen during the game to good use.

Most coaches hate "randoms." That's a word that describes times when everyone is scrambling around and not making high percentage plays. These situations cannot always be prevented, and it is during these times that a very high level of communication takes place through reading a teammate's mannerisms and using physical signals such as simple eye contact or head movements that insinuate some movement that's about to be made. This is the time when the game gets to be very invigorating and rewarding for players who have been through so much together over many years. When we are all in-sync, the game becomes a thing of effortless beauty. Some people call it momentum; I call it nirvana.

– Dave Cowens

Pick up almost any company's annual report, and you will probably find a line or two about their emphasis on communications, both internally among employees and externally with customers. Visit that organization. Do you sense that this espoused corporate value is real? I have often walked into companies and after a few interactions with employees in the lobby, I know there is a disconnect between what is said in the annual report about employees and the reality of how they treat their employees. I remember once going into the corporate office of a large retail company, picking up their annual report in the lobby and asking their receptionist about the values enumerated in their annual report. She said quickly, "Oh, we don't believe that stuff — it's just the annual report!"

Communication is one of the four core values at Northeast Delta Dental (NEDD). We believe that effective communication is essential for our continued success as a great place to work and a stellar place to do business for all customers, dentists and employees.

A key element of NEDD's internal communication process is what we call transparency, and transparency is one of the keys to remarkable success. As with most award-winning companies, at NEDD there exists open and honest communication within the entire organization — upward and downward, CEO to frontline employees, CEO to Board of Directors, and even Board of Directors directly to employees. For instance, preparing for NEDD Board meetings involves good planning and good communication. I prepare for Board meetings a lot like a football coach prepares for the next big game, with a game plan and a total focus on detail, trying to anticipate any question a Board member may ask. We have created

> **We believe that effective communication is essential for our continued success as a great place to work and a stellar place to do business.**

an online Board of Directors portal and discussion forum process, where management can answer Board members' questions online in advance, so that boardroom discussion can remain strategic and policy-oriented. This has built a great deal of trust between our Boards and our leadership.

We have a true open door policy at Northeast Delta Dental. The CEO and the entire management team are totally accessible. We always welcome employees into our offices to discuss anything, from the corporate vision, the competitive marketplace, customer concerns and/or home life balance (to the extent that employees are willing to share the trials and tribulations of their home life).

We take this transparency to heart — believing that information should literally be in plain sight. It is important that employees see the open door policy in order to feel it. To foster this, meeting room doors in our buildings have clear glass panels, so employees can see that nothing happens behind closed doors.

Our facility design enhances our open and transparent communication. Every employee was involved and engaged in the process of designing our One Delta Drive facility, first through brainstorming and benchmarking best practices, and later by serving on the design, planning or implementation teams. An idea from brainstorming that we put into practice was placing the CEO's office in the middle of the building. As employees walk by to get from one side of the building to the other, they say hello to me. This facilitates communications, lets me keep my finger on the pulse of the organization and provides what I like to call the "stop-and-tarry" approach that helps me to get to know all employees.

I constantly get positive comments from people outside the company telling me how our employees always know what is going on — that walking in the NEDD lobby is like walking into a fresh green forest, meaning they sense the environment is alive, friendly and genuine. As mentioned, a cross-functional team planned and coordinated for almost an entire year to create our new building design, which facilitated open communication, workflow, open landscaping, low walls and the importance of the right living space size (31,000 square feet at our One Delta Drive headquarters). Sir Richard Branson, who is best known as the founder of the Virgin Group of more than 400 companies, emphasizes that he tries to have only 100 to a maximum of 150 people working in any one building so they all get to know one another. He believes that having a building that size provides flexibility and facilitates the communication an organization needs to give people the freedom to work and be their best. This is the approach we took at our One Delta Drive building and again at our Two Delta Drive building. Our famous Root Canal tunnel running under Delta Drive physically and psychologically connects the buildings. I have found similar experiences in having 100 people in each of our two buildings. This provides us the appropriate building experience, helps improve work processes, and enhances communication.

The greatest and most cherished compliment I have received as a CEO is that I am the same person in the boardroom as I am in the mailroom. And it is true. I am equally comfortable and at peace in the boardroom as I am in the mailroom, and I talk the same way and give the same messages. I can effectively communicate with business leaders, NEDD Board members, and political leaders as easily as I can with frontline employees. In addition to the collegial things (family, children, school, weather and sports) that human beings chat about, the broad initiatives and issues I talk about, in both the boardroom and the mailroom, include future planning, daily challenges, financial results, performance expectations, and progress, as well as trends in the marketplace and the insurance industry. This is one way I try to share information and make it transparent to all.

People at NEDD understand that bad things can happen to companies, relationships and people when issues and problems are not addressed and resolved. We would much rather that people speak to us and make their case, even if they walk away disappointed with the result, than to not have had their say or day in court. Indecision and pent-up feelings cause premature death to people — and companies — due to the unnecessary stress and distraction that the unknown and unspoken creates.

In addition to transparency, a key aspect of communication is what I call tone or voice. I am not an overly talkative person but when playing a sports game such as basketball, like Dave Cowens, I shout signals all the time to help my teammates do their jobs better and to keep from being injured. A voice is a very powerful tool and is the most distinctive trait a person has. The thing I miss most about not having my father alive is listening to his voice, which could reassure, soothe, provoke and instruct in the simplest of ways at times. Just as we recognize the voices of our friends and family members, so employees recognize the voices of their managers or leaders. If I, as CEO, and my direct reports on the senior leadership team speak with one voice, people will find our communications clear and convincing. If we use the same language, the same illustrations, the same strategic metaphors, our communications will be much more effective than if we each wing it. As Dave said in his example, if the top leaders or coaches speak at "random" we will not have the high level of communication we need to be effective.

It is so important to build credibility with your employees and teammates by following the well-known adage: say what you mean and mean what you say. Consistent behavior and delivery on your promises adds to leadership's credibility.

Max DePree says in his book, *Leadership is an Art*, that one of the most important things the leader of a company must do is to help define reality, so employees understand the current environment and understand where the corporation is heading. In Professor Annabel Beerel's essay, "To Lead or Mislead," she emphasizes, "The primary task of leadership is to face reality." Dr. Beerel takes it further by indicating that "…every time we avoid, defer, negate, substitute, or create fantasy realities or even 'half-realities' we are misleading." Thus, NEDD has worked to communicate honestly about a new reality in the healthcare insurance world, the Patient Protection and Affordable Care Act (ACA).

The ACA, passed in March 2010, turned our insurance world upside down by potentially de-coupling benefits choices from employers. We, at NEDD, had to be ready if we were to survive and thrive. In June 2012, the United States Supreme Court ruled the ACA constitutional, and President Obama's re-election re-affirmed its validity. Whether or not we supported all of the objectives of the ACA, it was a reality and it was crucial that all employees in the company understood its implications to NEDD. Because of our robust scenario planning and communications, NEDD was totally prepared to deal with its implications, including addressing the retail dental insurance market. As we approach most things, we view the ACA as an opportunity to enhance our oral health mission — not an obstruction to it.

To deal with the realities of the ACA, transforming NEDD from a business-to-business to a business-to-consumer enterprise, it was necessary to coach employees on the need for change caused by our new reality. Change is difficult because of how our brains are wired. Senior leadership acknowledged that it is a natural reaction to resist change. The first step to take was organizational awareness — telling the truth about the new reality brought on by the ACA, that it was here to stay and would impact the company, but that we could turn it into a positive force. We explained the ACA as a cycle of renewal for the company — accepting and understanding the new fact that dental benefits might no longer be linked to employment benefits. Thus, we needed to direct our oral health message to the individual consumer through kiosks, radio and other business-to-consumer media. This might lead to innovations to address the new realities of the ACA and thus new opportunities. As an organization, we agreed to move on and find a way to succeed in this new healthcare world.

Back in 1996, we took this same approach to using our communications to define a new reality with the introduction of our world famous Guarantee Of Service Excellence^{SM} (GOSE) program. *(See Chapter 9: Please Your Fans for more details on GOSE.)* At that time, no other insurance company in New Hampshire and only one other insurance company in the United States (that being Delta Dental of Massachusetts, where I instituted the same program during my tenure there) had a universal guarantee. It was important that employees understood the value of the universal guarantee, both from the continuous improvement perspective and from the marketing perspective. Our GOSE program epitomizes my belief that it is effective business practice to under-promise but over-deliver.

Implementing the GOSE program was a total company effort that required leadership to deal with employees' resistance to change. I believed this would be the propelling force of NEDD's cultural transformation from a sleepy little-known New Hampshire company to a prominent, positive force in New Hampshire, Maine and Vermont. To achieve this, GOSE had to be the focus of our External Affairs campaign, but marketing employees were not quite sure if they wanted to place all our then-limited corporate resource eggs in one basket. Once again, the key to dealing with the natural human reaction to resist change was to keep communication open and to establish cross-functional work groups in which all employees participated. Ultimately, there was total employee buy-in, and GOSE became — and to this day continues to be — a great source of employee pride.

Another important aspect of communication is clarity or speaking plainly. As referenced earlier, the biggest compliment I receive is that I am the same person in the boardroom as I am in the mailroom, and that is because I speak plainly. I first learned this from my grandmother who described a colander, in broken English, as "water go through, spaghetti stay." As a little boy, I knew right away what to retrieve from the cabinet even though I didn't know the name of the utensil.

Many years later, my toddler twin sons described a car carrier as "cars up on a truck." Looking for car carriers kept them from crying. Whenever I needed some peace and quiet in the car, I would announce that we are going to look for "cars up on a truck." My sons knew right away what I was talking about.

We never want a situation where a neighbor or friend asks a NEDD employee about the ACA (or some other relevant corporate headline) and our employee is unable to explain the implications of that corporate headline. Therefore, we have created and regularly use various methods and channels for communication. We have found face-to-face communications to be important to strategy implementation (such as GOSE and the ACA), and thus long ago we established our quarterly All Colleagues Meetings, which I have mentioned several times. These are meetings where all Northeast Delta Dental employees assemble in a conference room for two hours. Preparing for these meetings is a long process. As CEO, I need to develop a strategic agenda and messaging that every employee can understand easily. I have two hours in front of all employees every three months. It is an opportunity to share our strategic vision and have a question and answer period. I also get to help develop other employees' talents by encouraging others to make presentations in front of all their colleagues. On the one hand, this is an expensive meeting in that everyone is away from their core job for two hours; on the other hand, what an opportunity to share ideas and corporate plans with colleagues!

There are numerous other methods we use to communicate and keep everyone informed. These include global email messages from the CEO to all employees following board meetings. I also send routine informational CEO emails to keep everyone in the loop or just to touch base. Monthly we publish our internal employee newsletter, *Team Power*, and I have Coffee with the Coach get-togethers with a mix of veteran and new employees. When needed we conduct the "Big Tour" of the claims flow process as part of our on-boarding process for new employees. Connecting with the Coach is an informal meeting with managers and the CEO. There are also various other employee meeting forums for financial presentations, new product presentations and new direction presentations.

Every department holds regular staff meetings. These provide an opportunity for managers to tell employees what's going on in the corporation and for employees to provide input and feedback. We're fortunate to have valued long-term employees who bring priceless institutional memory and history to our culture; they've been there, done that and know what works and what doesn't. The combination of our seasoned, experienced employees coupled with new employees who bring us fresh ideas and new worldly and industry perspectives truly makes NEDD a juggernaut in the dental insurance space in New Hampshire, Maine and Vermont.

Up to this point, I've focused on internal communications with our employees or teammates. External communication with customers or other stakeholders is also essential to success. With customers, as with internal employees, the principles of transparency, consistency, clarity, and the use of various methods are all important.

After the ACA passed, to facilitate our ability to sell dental insurance direct to consumers, we worked with another Delta Dental Member Company to promote DeltaDentalCoversMe.com. This is an online website for dental insurance, which can be the Travelocity or Amazon equivalent for consumer-driven healthcare purchases. Directing oral health messages to the consumer is, of course, a different process than business-to-business transactions. Direct-to-consumer marketing requires using social media and other channels not previously needed by NEDD. For example, NEDD's recent introduction of selling dental insurance through kiosks, radio shows, TV commercials, fleet advertising (ads on the panels of tractor trailer trucks), and stadium naming ("Northeast Delta Dental Stadium" in Manchester, New Hampshire) are all direct-to-consumer strategies. In addition, NEDD coordinated ACA educational conferences and developed user friendly ACA navigational brochures.

We also established an Internet-based product through DeltaDentalCoversMe.com to make it easy for the consumer to purchase a cost effective dental program. In a direct-to-consumer world, branding is important, but so is price, so we developed four dental plan designs that fell well below the magical fifty-dollar-per-month benchmark. Direct-to-consumer is a new opportunity, not an obstacle, and has actually rejuvenated our corporate creative juices!

I would like to caution you not to let social media and the fast pace at which information is exchanged erode your ability to communicate with clarity and precision. The value of social media is that it provides many ways to connect and share information, but it can also be a distraction. Social media must always complement, and not replace, face-to-face communication. Connecting with people through one-on-one conversations is still the most valuable form of communication, and I encourage students that I mentor to build relationships that way. Social media's value must be balanced with the potential for distraction, and even sometimes disaster, but social media does have a value and is not going away, though its form will doubtlessly change over time. At Northeast Delta Dental, we have a team of employees from different departments who handle our Facebook page, our Twitter account, Google rankings and our YouTube presence. I also have a ghostwriter (Barbara McLaughlin) who helps prepare some of my CEO blogs.

I have described the various ways we communicate with our employees and customers. Now, with that said, it is very important that we measure the effectiveness of our communications. Those of you who are familiar with the Baldrige Performance Excellence Program and its many principles of good management understand that, to some extent, you are what you measure. To obtain insights into how our employees feel about our culture and communications, our Human Resources Department, headed by our Vice President Connie Roy-Czyzowski, coordinates focus groups, and the results are written up so that the employees' individual comments are kept confidential. We also get feedback through our informal Coffee with the Coach sessions throughout the year. I have obtained a number of valuable improvement ideas from these over the years, such as the need to improve our phone system and ideas for our new buildings. So, these have been a success for all of us.

Every two years, we assess how employees view the culture of our company through an employee Strategic Alignment Survey (SAS) that is used internationally and provides important benchmarks. One hundred percent of employees participate in the survey, which includes measuring how effective we are in our communications. The chart below is a twelve-year snapshot of how our employees evaluate us overall based on the satisfaction survey. As you can see, NEDD sets the bar for those companies all across the country that participate in the same survey process. We are told by the SAS consultants that other United States companies lament, "Who is that company in Concord, New Hampshire that gets these high rankings that the rest can only dream to attain?"

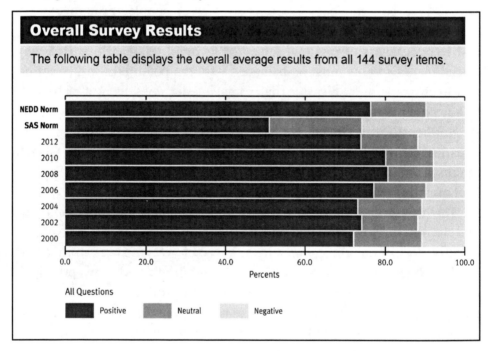

We also evaluate how our Board of Directors members view our communications. Since 2005, we have conducted a biannual survey to query the opinions of the members of our three Boards of Directors and Trustees in Maine, New Hampshire, and Vermont regarding the effectiveness and alignment of the current governance in support of the NEDD strategy. The results of these surveys have always been very positive.

If asked to sum up what I have learned about communicating well, I would have to say that it is almost impossible to communicate too widely, too often, or too honestly. We work on communicating well to everyone, from our Boards of Directors to our newest employees. We communicate all the time through meetings, newsletters, blogs, and daily encounters. And we always, always tell the truth as simply and clearly as we know how.

THE BIG RED FACTOR

All organizations, in business or in sports, require a good strategy or game plan that is properly implemented to be totally successful. Everyone in the organization is part of the game and vital to success. And, to keep everyone working together to win the game, great communication is a necessity. I believe that game-winning communications require transparency, consistency, clarity, and the ability to define reality persuasively. Also, it is important to use a variety of communication methods — especially face-to-face communications — to tell the story effectively. Finally, it is important to measure or monitor how well the communications are working and to improve them as needed. In short, the Big Red Factor for communicating to win is to make the total commitment to communicate honestly, regularly, clearly, and persuasively through many channels with teammates and all stakeholders.

Chapter 9

Please Your Fans

"An acre of performance is worth a whole world of promise."

– Red Auerbach

In sports, winning begets a generational following that you build on with the younger folks. As a basketball player, I had little to do with the business of keeping old and gaining new customers. All I did was do my job on the court, which — if it was good enough and we won — meant more people became interested in watching or listening to the Celtics play.

Red Auerbach was not big on promotions and elaborate public relations campaigns. Heck, he didn't even like having cheerleaders, dancers, mascots, and all the music and video displays they have today.

The organization always had us doing preseason clinics in and around Boston to drum up support. The team would travel to all parts of New England and be part of school openings by conducting team scrimmages and clinics at newly built gymnasiums. They would do eight to twelve of these each preseason to promote the team and break the monotony of training camp. They usually traveled by car with Red driving along with a few of the players using their cars to transport the team to the various sites. We also did newspaper and TV interviews to stay in the forefront of their minds.

– Dave Cowens

A huge goal for every sports team — beside winning games — is to fill all the seats in the venue. Every team wants as many fans cheering for them as possible. That means having season ticket holders who are loyal and renew their season tickets every year. It also means having a waiting list of other fans who are eager to buy tickets and even become season subscribers. Businesses are the same. They all want lots of loyal fans or customers. And, to make up for the customers who don't or can't renew, they want to attract new fans or customers.

As Dave's story says, every team has to work proactively to build its fan base. Winning is a huge part of that, but if a team treated its fans shabbily, they would not return. And, as is often seen with minor league baseball teams, it is possible to fill seats even in losing seasons if the team shows the fans a good enough time with events for the children, great food and so on.

There's an old song sung around many a campfire that goes, "Make new friends, but keep the old. One is silver and the other gold." That's what sports teams and businesses both care about. They need to keep the old friends (the "gold" who are loyal customers and fans) and make new friends (the "silver" who are eager to become new customers and fans). Research has long held that retaining existing customers is usually more profitable than the costs associated with having to attract and acquire new customers to replace a lost customer. We have proven this at NEDD. You need both gold and silver: the gold, for your reputation and profitability; the silver, because a company that is not growing can fall into a downward spiral and not be infused with new challenging customers that push the company to new heights.

As you learned at the beginning of this book, I actually first met Dave Cowens in 1970 when I was a freshman in high school. Forty-one years later, we reconnected at a conference where Dave was the featured speaker to provide inspirational and leadership ideas. In Dave's speech, he mentioned the concept of "gold and silver;" gold being retaining current customers and keeping them delighted, and silver meaning gaining new customers. Dave and I have discussed this since the conference, and he shared with me some of his experiences after leaving the Celtics.

"When my playing career ended, I was privileged to get involved with exemplary businesses and connected with business leaders who believed in many of the same principles as Northeast Delta Dental. For this book, I was able to draw from not only my athletic experiences, but also from these remarkable business contacts. I learned the importance of investing time in nurturing current customers and donors using handwritten notes during various times of the year to emphasize that current customers (gold) are not to be taken for granted.

"I had a similar experience in serving on the Olympic Bank Board in the 1980s. Olympic Bank nurtured long-term customers and would work with these "gold" customers, even in trying times. We did not want them go out of business so we extended their credit through a difficult economic downturn. We knew they were good business people in the good times so we felt with a little patience they would once again be prosperous. You wouldn't stop throwing the ball to your best shooter just because he was in a scoring slump."

As I was listening to Dave speak, what came to mind was our GOSE (Guarantee Of Service Excellence^SM) program that has brought Northeast Delta Dental so much success over the years. GOSE is nationally acclaimed for the breakthrough positive change it has made in the insurance industry with regard to service. Because of our GOSE, NEDD is well known in Maine, New Hampshire and Vermont for the outstanding quality of service to its customers. GOSE has been featured in such books and articles as Professor Christopher W. L. Hart's *Extraordinary Guarantees,* Tom Peters' "On Achieving Excellence" newsletter, as well as John Tschohl's book (with a similar title) *Achieving Excellence through Customer Service.* It was also used in a business case study at the University of Virginia Darden School of Business. If you are interested in learning more about the power of service guarantees, you should pick up a copy of Dr. Hart's book, *Extraordinary Guarantees*. While it was published back in 1993, it still stands the test of time as the seminal piece on service guarantees.

> **Giving customer service that stands out from competitors is all about getting the details right and, sometimes, about how well we recover from our mistakes.**

NEDD's GOSE links to the gold and silver concept. GOSE is set up to attract new customers (silver) and also set up to retain existing customers (gold). I like to tell my colleagues that if they are going to be unabashedly compulsive about one thing, I want it to be about the service they provide. Giving customer service that stands out from competitors is all about getting the details right and, sometimes, about how well we recover from our mistakes. I also tell my colleagues that it's important to strive for perfection, because the effort pushes us closer to that goal. However, we must also recognize that we will all make an error here or there. The primary way that we deal with service glitches is through our comprehensive service guarantee program. Here are the details of our seven-part GOSE.

We Guarantee Our Service

Northeast Delta Dental is committed to providing exceptional service to all its customers. To emphasize our commitment, our *Guarantee Of Service Excellence*[SM] program guarantees the following seven major areas of service and reinforces them with our comprehensive group refund policy.

Guarantee of Service Excellence

1	SMOOTH IMPLEMENTATION TO NORTHEAST DELTA DENTAL	Successful implementation will be determined by you through the results of a survey.	Refund: Your group will be reimbursed the administration fee charged for the second month of service per your contract.
2	EXCEPTIONAL CUSTOMER SERVICE	We will resolve inquiries immediately or guarantee an initial update within one business day.	Refund: Your group will be reimbursed $50 per occurrence.
3	QUICK PROCESSING OF CLAIMS	During the course of a contract year, 90 percent of your group's accurately completed claim forms will be processed within fifteen calendar days.	Refund: Your group will be reimbursed the administration fee for its last month of service per your contract.
4	NO INAPPROPRIATE BILLING BY PARTICIPATING DENTISTS	Patients will not be charged for more than the appropriate co-payments at the time of service or for any difference between a participating dentist's submitted fee and our approved amount.	Refund: Your group will be reimbursed $50 per occurrence.
5	ACCURATE AND QUICK TURNAROUND OF IDENTIFICATION CARDS	Accurate identification cards will be mailed within fifteen calendar days upon receipt of a completed enrollment form or request.	Refund: Your group will be reimbursed $25 per pair of identification cards.
6	TIMELY EMPLOYEE BOOKLETS	Standard Plan Description Booklets and/or Outlines of Benefits will be mailed within fifteen calendar days of request, finalized benefits change, or receipt of signed contract.	Refund: Your group will be reimbursed $50 per occurrence.
7	MARKETING SERVICE CONTACTS	You will receive at least two marketing service contacts during a contract term.	Refund: Your group will be reimbursed $50 per occurrence.

Guarantee #1 of GOSE says that if you are currently not a NEDD customer, but switch to us, we will return one month's administration fee if your transition to NEDD is not totally smooth. That is the silver feature of GOSE — attracting new customers.

And, significantly, the determination of whether the transition is totally smooth is up to the customer! What we learned through market research is that many prospective customers of NEDD wanted to come to NEDD. They were aware of our better dental plan designs, dentist networks and exemplary service. However, decision makers at these prospective companies were unwilling to stick their necks out to convert to NEDD. The decision makers feared that if they made the wrong decision and the conversion went badly, their employees would be upset and their jobs would be on the line. Guarantee #1 reduces the risk for the decision makers to move their business to NEDD because, should the conversion not be smooth (which is the call of the decision maker), NEDD rewards the group with one month of administrative expense relief. These can be large dollar amounts, so we are putting real money where our GOSE mouth is!

NEDD's GOSE #1 has helped us beat the competition, because no bureaucratic insurance company is willing to put hundreds of thousands of dollars on the line when the decision of whether a conversion is smooth or not is left totally to the discretion and opinion of the customer. The "silver" new customers since the inception of GOSE have resulted in NEDD's market share increasing from 20 percent in our three states to 60 percent in Maine, and 75 percent in both New Hampshire and Vermont.

With regard to keeping current gold customers, our other six guarantees, such as #2: Calls Returned Within One Business Day and #3: Quick Processing of Claims, all relate to existing companies that we serve. They deal with daily service standards that we want to provide to our customers. We do not wait for customers to complain but proactively apologize and offer amends when we fail to meet those standards. For example, we returned over $13,000 to the City of Manchester when one year we processed 89.96 percent of claims within fifteen days and did not meet our 90 percent GOSE standard. We did not round up to 90 percent as some might have done. As a result, the City of Manchester has become a customer for life and a loyal ambassador for the Northeast Delta Dental brand. Because of GOSE, we have built an extremely loyal customer base. We have crushed the competition, as NEDD retains 97 to 99 percent of its employer customers in a group insurance industry where the average retention rate is 80 percent.

A final GOSE promise worth mentioning is GOSE #7: Each Group Will Receive at least Two Marketing Service Contacts During a Contract Year. In addition to impeccable service, Northeast Delta Dental has found that this person-to-person communication has created a trust between NEDD and its group customers. We find that these personal contacts have focused us on all three of the three tenets recommended by Ernst & Young: loyalty, satisfaction, and retention.

Retaining current "gold" customers, of course, is generally more profitable than bringing in new customers because insurance firms almost always have to price aggressively in order to attract a new customer. At NEDD, we never price at a loss, or "buy" business one year only to recoup our losses the following year with extreme increases in premium to that group. We win new business because of GOSE and our resulting reputation.

You can see this has built our financial strength, even in a troubled economy. NEDD has been widely recognized with many awards, and equally important, the financial and marketing results of the corporation have been outstanding. In 2010, the corporation's growth in our surplus (revenues minus expenses), enterprise-wide, was nearly $1 million, and in 2012 it was over $7.6 million. From the inception of GOSE in 1995 to now, corporate reserves have grown from $8.5 million to $95 million in 2013.

I mentioned earlier that GOSE helps us recover from our mistakes, which, like every other organization, we do inevitably make. In a customer-driven world, service recovery becomes an important corporate strategy. For those of you interested in learning more about service recovery, I recommend the Ernst & Young document, "Customer Disappointment: How to Recover from Mistakes." It is worthwhile and is an outstanding recipe for how to capitalize on errors.

When we make mistakes, GOSE payments are proactively sent to the customer. They don't have to ask for the refund. But even better, in addition to keeping our promise, we also explain to customers what process improvement we made so the same mistake won't occur again. This total trust brings us the 97 to 99 percent retention and is why NEDD continues to thrive. It's also why our mission to spread access to good oral health has been successful, growing from 301,000 covered lives in northern New England in 1995 when I arrived at NEDD to over 750,000 lives in 2013.

Organizations that focus on serving the customers — that care about the gold and the silver — also create a beautiful circle because employees want to work for a company that's acclaimed as an industry leader. At NEDD, we value energetic employees who are focused on their work and pay attention to the details of pleasing customers. Satisfied and self-actualizing employees are more productive and focused on getting the job done, so we treat employees the way we want them to treat the customers they serve, and it shows in our customer satisfaction, loyalty and retention.

In addition to our GOSE, NEDD conducts customer research to be sure we are on track and are continuing to meet our customers' expectations or needs. Among other things, we want to be sure that our seven GOSE guarantees are enough to set us well above the competition and that no competitor is achieving our levels of service. Some years back, for instance, we conducted focus groups to determine whether we needed to tweak our guarantees — nope! We also conduct many customer surveys to track our customer satisfaction and loyalty. Through the hard work of our employees, we remain highly rated with an excellent reputation.

We have never gotten off track with GOSE as the program recently celebrated its fifteenth anniversary. While other companies try various quality initiatives and dabble in guarantees, no national insurance company has stayed the course. No competitor has had the guts to copy the guarantee universally. Some competitors will copy the guarantee for a key account, but never for their entire book of business. Another might adopt one or two features for parts of their business, but never the entire guarantee. Competitive insurance companies are afraid that a universal guarantee will be too costly, both in terms of payouts and building the infrastructure to support it. Competitors don't understand the continuous improvement nature of the program: refunds are actually investments in your customers and your infrastructure that will pay long-term dividends because they build customer satisfaction and loyalty. The guarantees help to improve your organization, building long-term trust, securing life-long customers, increasing positive word of mouth and leading to more customers!

THE BIG RED FACTOR

In Dave's story about the Celtics under Red Auerbach, he makes the point that winning, or providing what customers hope for, is important. But even the Celtics in the old days before cheerleaders and crowd-pleasing extras, went out of their way to build relationships with the community of fans. We all need to do that: make sure we are giving our customers what they want and then go above and beyond. To paraphrase famous football coach and Hall of Famer Bill Parcells, what matters is your record and performance, not your excuses. I suggest you be as single-minded about pleasing your customers, about meeting their needs, about perfection as Red Auerbach and Big Red were. You would think that in this economic climate every business and sports team would recognize the value of exceptional customer service and strive to provide it as they compete for customers. But all of us can think of poor service we have received where the organizations just didn't seem to care. They don't apologize, and they don't seem to try to recover from their mistakes or prevent them from happening in the future. Even if you don't provide a written guarantee, you might try an unwritten one that is known inside your organization. That makes it clear to all employees what your service standards are and then empowers them to make things right for customers if the organization occasionally can't live up to those standards. You will find, as we did, that you retain more loyal customers (the gold) and attract more new customers (the silver).

Fourth Quarter

"The best way to forget one's self is to look at the world with attention and love."

– Red Auerbach

Chapter 10

Pay Attention to the Score

"If winning isn't everything, why do they keep score?"

– Vince Lombardi

When I coached in the Continental Basketball Association for the Bay State Bombardiers, they had a different way of measuring the outcome of the game and your team record. Each game had seven points that were up for grabs. The game would reward a team one point for each of the four quarters it won and three points for having the most points upon completion of the contest. Therefore, the winning team would have to amass at least four points (such as by winning at least one quarter as well as having the most points at completion) in order to win the game. The losing team could earn up to three points in that game.

The scores from each game were recorded and added to each team's total for the season. The winners of each division were decided by how many points were accumulated throughout the season. This was an interesting way to keep score because it rewarded a high level of consistent play throughout the entire game by incentivizing a team to win each period. Therefore, all end-of-period plays were of greater importance in close games, which kept the competitiveness at a higher level all game long.

The CBA had a rule that players could not foul out. When a player had reached his allotted six fouls for the game, the coach could elect to keep the player in the game. However, the penalty for taking advantage of that rule was that if that player fouled again the other team would get to shoot two free throws plus keep possession of the ball. As you can surmise from these rules, there were more coaching decisions made during a CBA game than are made in an NBA game. Also, the temptation of players to coast during the game and then step it up in the fourth quarter is diminished, making for a better product.

I learned to take this newfound attention to detail into my NBA coaching philosophy: I instilled into my players that every possession counts. It is interesting to note that Phil Jackson and George Karl both cut their coaching teeth in the CBA and have had outstanding careers in the NBA. Phil coached eleven NBA championship-winning teams, breaking Red Auerbach's seemingly untouchable record of nine championships. Perhaps Phil's and George's (number seven in all time career wins) great coaching was due partly in that they had to experiment with play execution more often as CBA coaches in end of period situations.

Many coaches devote a segment of every practice to special situations, which are determined by score and time. For example, here's a situation: two seconds left, we have possession, sideline out of bounds play, and we are down one point. The teams are divided up, and the head coach and the top assistant take teams. One takes offense; the other takes defense. These times in practice are normally very competitive, and the players are highly focused.

– Dave Cowens

We have all heard basketball commentators talk about how a team's players seem to work extra hard during the fourth quarter. We've all seen games where the play seems almost leisurely in the middle of the game and then ratchets up a notch as the clock ticks down and the final buzzer gets closer. Even in a play-off series, it seems as if the play is most intense in the final game. Why is that? Dave says he thinks it's because of the focus on the clock: "You see, I don't believe that the level of competitiveness rises for everyone late in the game, only that more importance is placed on this period of time in the game because it becomes more finite."

Some others suggest that we could chalk it up to human nature, but I think it's more than that. I think, as Dave's story suggests, that it's because we have two vital measures —

> In business, as I often say to my colleagues, "Let's not confuse activity with accomplishment." The score matters!

score and time — that make it clear to all the players that they need to hustle because there are no do-overs. When the game is over, it's over. There's no point in saving energy during the fourth quarter, because there will be plenty of time to rest after the final buzzer.

I remember watching the 1976 NBA finals playoffs between the Boston Celtics and the Phoenix Suns. (I was a sophomore at Harvard so we all watched games on TV in those days.) This was the famous fifth game in the series, with triple overtime, an NBA classic that continues to be re-aired on television. This was the game where the Celtics kept blowing big leads and the Suns kept bouncing back. What I remember most about this series was the announcer, Brent Musburger, talking about how much that "red head" (meaning Dave Cowens) hustled. (Yes, this is the same Brent Musburger, thirty-seven years later, who made a controversial comment about the beauty of Miss Alabama USA at the 2013 Alabama versus Notre Dame national championship football game.) Musburger's comment about Dave Cowens in 1976 was well received by the public. Who could argue with Dave's hustle?

As Dave did in that famous game and throughout his career, my colleagues and I at Northeast Delta Dental (NEDD) always try to outwork the competition. We keep our eyes focused on our goals. We are driven to hustle by both the fear of failure and the desire to succeed. In business, as I often say to my colleagues, "Let's not confuse activity with accomplishment." The score matters!

I think NEDD has accomplished a lot and scored well. We have hired the right people and then trained and empowered them so they can perform well. We look after our people and reward and recognize them so they are happy to be working at NEDD. We communicate honestly and consistently so we are trusted inside and outside of our organization by employees and customers. We promise and deliver great service to our customers. And, the result — as measured through the satisfaction of our employees and customers, our renewal or retention rate of employees and customers, our new customer growth rate and market share, and our financials — is that we are a high-scoring, game-winning company.

I think that one very important reason for NEDD's success is that we measure every important aspect of our business. Let me say that again because it is important: we measure every important aspect of our business. Just as basketball teams are measured by their scores, the clock, and many other revealing statistics, we at NEDD are measured by what we call our "balanced scorecard." As the old adage goes, "What gets measured gets managed."

We did not invent this balanced scorecard concept. (It was first written about by Robert S. Kaplan and David P. Norton in the *Harvard Business Review* in 1992 as, "The Balanced Scorecard: Measures that Drive Performance," and they and others since then have produced numerous articles and books on the benefits and best practices of using scorecards to measure and motivate great performance.) But we are great believers in and users of the balanced scorecard.

It has been my experience, at NEDD and by observing or examining other successful companies that compete for the Granite State Quality Council Award, and the Massachusetts equivalent, that a good company becomes what it measures. All the best organizations begin their choice of measures by thinking about their mission and strategy because that's what is most important to success.

It is essential that an enterprise measure the right things. It is surprisingly easy to measure the wrong things. Some organizations measure unimportant things — perhaps because the measures are easy to obtain or because the measures have always been used. Still other organizations fail to measure the things that really matter — such as customer and employee satisfaction and loyalty. Other organizations sometimes measure counter-productive things. For instance, you may have heard about the firm that knew from a survey that callers to the helpline liked to have their questions answered promptly. So the firm chose to measure how many seconds each call lasted, with fewer seconds being better than more seconds. The result — you guessed it — was that the phone reps couldn't end the calls quickly enough — even if they hadn't fully answered all the customers' questions. As a result of that counter-productive measure, satisfaction plummeted.

At NEDD, we make sure we are measuring the right things. We begin with a collaborative process that involves all employees, most especially front-line employees closest to the customer, in the strategic planning process. The process culminates with a strategic retreat with the NEDD Board of Directors to ensure we have picked the right strategy for the corporation.

The Board and management understand Einstein's famous quote, "Not everything that can be counted counts, and not everything that counts can be measured." Nevertheless, the directors and managers translate the strategic objectives developed at the planning retreat into the measures that we think best describe what is important.

To communicate our strategic goals and the related measures, we divide our balanced scorecard into four "perspectives." These are Financial, Customer, Internal, and Innovation/Learning/Growth. The figure that follows gives a snapshot of one of our corporate scorecards. Each department has its own equivalent balanced scorecard, which feeds into the corporate balanced scorecard.

Northeast Delta Dental's Balanced Scorecard
Team Share Incentive Plan

OBJECTIVES	MEASURES	1/1/12 – 12/31/12		
		WEIGHT	TARGET	PERFORMANCE
FINANCIAL Perspective - 40%				
Five-year average combined ratio of 99% or better	Total Claims & Admin/ Total Revenue Annual Target w/DTC: 100.3%	10%	100.3%	99.7%
Control administrative costs to achieve nine objectives	Total admin percentage (excludes DTC) Annual Target: 9.7%	10%	9.7%	10.08%
Subscriber Growth	Subscribers from New Groups Annual Target: 12,600	10%	12,600	10,206
Customer Retention	Group-based subscriber retention net of state plans (100% retention) and Delta USA transfers	10%	95%	93.8%
CUSTOMER Perspective - 20%				
Quality Service	Annual overall satisfaction score for subscribers/decision maker/dentists & dental office staff	10%	At least 85% world class benchmark	Later This Year
Network Accessibility	Satisfaction ratings from subscribers and purchasers on access to participating dentists	10%	Attain over 85% world class benchmark and track individual state satisfaction results for more than five points fluctuation	Later This Year
INTERNAL Perspective - 20%				
Prompt claims turnaround	Claims processed within 15 calendar days of receipt	5%	90% as guaranteed in GOSE	99.8%
Accurate claims processing	% monetary accuracy rate meet or exceed DDPA standards	5%	99%	100%
Best in class customer service	Abandonment rate	5%	10% or less	9%
	Speed of answer	5%	45 seconds or less	119
INNOVATION, LEARNING, & GROWTH Perspective - 20%				
Hire and retain capable employees	Turnover %	5%	Less than industry average of 9.2%	3.87%
	Productivity (Claims/FTE)	5%	8,590	8,828
Select, implement, and maintain technology to support corporation	Aggregate system availability	5%	Better than 99%	99.8%
Employee alignment with company mission and values	Strategic alignment survey results, (survey done every two years; results used on BSC for two years)	5%	At least 10 points over strategic alignment survey benchmark 63%	73%

COMPANY INITIATIVES

Our 2012 Theme: "Ready for Retail"

Preparing for Direct to Consumer market:

- Direct to Consumer (DTC) Marketing Plan — 7/1/2012 - Completed
- CRM Software Implemented — 8/1/2012 - Completed Target Implementation
- New Individual Product Launched — 10/1/2012 - Completed
- Viable Stand-Alone PPO Network — 12/31/2012 - Completed (achieved 20% PPO network)

At NEDD, we have blended the human need for rewards for individual skills with rewards for contributions as a team member. Our strategy and measures are cascaded and aligned through our divisions and departments down to the individual level. Everyone in the company, from the CEO on down, receives a team bonus based on the four key balanced scorecard metrics. Within each of these metrics are objectives and measures to which everyone in the company contributes.

We have a "teamshare" approach that encourages everyone in the corporation to row in the same direction. The teamshare bonus is given to everyone in the corporation if we make our goals. In addition to this bonus, each employee is evaluated on his or her individual contribution based on semi-annual and annual performance reviews. We reinforce teamwork and incentives for teamwork via carefully planned human resource training programs that encourage managers, directors, and vice presidents to be more like coaches than referees because coaches want their players to shine.

At NEDD and other role model companies, each employee has a sense of ownership in the organization's success. That in turn provides the internal motivation to continue to do one's best for the success of the company team. "Ownership" can mean employee stock ownership in a public company, but at NEDD (where there are no stockholders), ownership means "buy in" and the feeling that "this is my company, and I want it to succeed." And because of how well our employees understand our scorecard and their individual goals, they can see how well we and they are progressing toward success.

To ensure that our balanced scorecard is understood and effective, we used the S.M.A.R.T. goal process (S.M.A.R.T. = specific, measurable, attainable, relevant, timely). Together, these are designed to recognize the accomplishments of the corporation and also recognize individual and divisional superior contributions. The chart following demonstrates how the S.M.A.R.T. goals process is deployed at Northeast Delta Dental, from individual to overall corporate.

Superior Performance	
Direct to Consumer (DTC) Implementation Timeline	
Direct to Consumer (DTC) Marketing Plan	**7/1/2012**
CRM Software Implemented	**8/1/2012**
New Individual Products Launched	**10/1/2012**
Viable Stand-Alone PPO Network	12/31/2012

Let me give you an idea of how powerful our balanced scorecard measures and goals are in helping our NEDD team pull together to achieve important things. In 2012, in anticipation of the Affordable Care Act's (ACA) radical changes in healthcare payments and insurance, NEDD realized it would have to sell Direct to Consumers (DTC) rather than just to employers. So it was vital to NEDD's strategy and success that we develop Customer Relationship Management (CRM) software, file with our regulators less expensive retail products, and build a Preferred Provider Organization (PPO) through active dentist recruiting. These 2012 S.M.A.R.T. goals were prominently displayed in posters and billboards across our corporate campus, discussed regularly at All Colleagues Meetings and our Board of Directors meetings, and published in our *Team Power* newsletter. At the September All Colleagues Meeting that year, we announced that we did not think we would achieve the PPO goal. Upon hearing that, employees took up the challenge, and we achieved this stretch goal. Publicizing the S.M.A.R.T. goals and having them everywhere, top of mind, were instrumental in the successful achievement of all of our ACA and DTC goals. This DTC poster, which communicates our S.M.A.R.T. goals program, was on display throughout our campus as a motivational tool to focus each employee on our goals.

2013 Strategic Initiatives Implementing Retail	
Prepared for Public Exchange Sales	10/1/13
Tri-State Average PPO Network at 25%	12/31/13
Individual/Family and Small Group Net Subscriber Increase of 8,000	12/31/13

Another, much earlier example, occurred when we first implemented our Guarantee Of Service Excellence[SM] or GOSE. Before we went live with GOSE, we ran in test mode and anticipated a certain level of payouts for failing to achieve the standards we promised or guaranteed to our customers. But once we went live, NEDD employees rose to the occasion and our actual performance was far above the test phase, meaning our actual customer refunds were less than expected. Indeed, we became what we measured, and as long as the enterprise is measuring the right items, the company is golden.

As CEO, I have personal or individual objectives — just as all our other staff members do. Mine focus on the essentials of leadership. One pet peeve of mine is the notion that no one who pays attention to detail can also be a visionary. I disagree. Sanford Weill, former CEO of Citigroup, summed it up well when he said, "Details create the big picture."

My personal goals as CEO emphasize both attention to detail and a concerted focus on achieving our mission and strategic goals. These are the factors considered by the NEDD Compensation Committee and then by our Boards of Directors as I am reviewed. These factors are based on Jim Collins' book, *Good to Great*, where he describes the traits of the highest level of leadership.

Do I foster an environment of innovation, development, agility, and growth?

Do I promote consideration, development, and implementation of diversification strategies and opportunities for continuous improvement to ensure the sustainability of NEDD well into the future?

Do I demonstrate an unyielding commitment to the corporate mission, vision, and values, including communication, quality, teamwork, and integrity?

Do I assure consistent focus on corporate priorities, opportunities, and key constituencies?

Do I demonstrate personal openness and dedication to professional development, respectful critique, and continuous improvement?

Do I attain and consistently re-earn "High Level Leadership" status?

I submit to you that if I can achieve these goals, paying attention to the details revealed through our balanced scorecard, and leading others toward our mission and strategic goals, then it's magical for our company! I understand that, as the CEO leader of a nationally acclaimed company, all of my personal achievements would mean little if NEDD was not successful. But NEDD is incredibly successful as measured by our balanced scorecard as a result of teamwork, board and management alignment, and our ability to plan for the future.

THE BIG RED FACTOR

Like sports teams, businesses must pay attention to their scores or measures to know how they are doing. Are they winning, and if not, how far behind the competition are they? It's important for

---

all organizations to have a balanced set of measures (a balanced scorecard) that reflects their definitions of winning because in the final analysis, what they measure becomes their management goal. Businesses can only manage what they measure.

A balanced scorecard of measures offers many advantages. The measures in the scorecard reflect what's strategically important to the organization — its ability to achieve its mission and strategic goals. The scorecard acts as a communication tool — like a scoreboard at a game — that lets everyone see in real time how the organization is doing. A balanced scorecard aligns everyone in the organization — from the CEO to the frontline and across all departments or divisions — in working toward shared goals. A balanced scorecard is a motivational tool when combined with recognition and rewards from the corporate to the individual level. And, a balanced scorecard is a management tool that allows leaders to adapt when a game plan or strategy may not be working and needs to be adjusted.

Postgame Highlights

"Success is the sum of paying attention to detail."

— Tom Raffio

Chapter 11

Success Is the Sum of Paying Attention to Detail

"If you think small things don't matter,
think of the last game you lost by one point."

– Author Unknown

After I finished my playing career, I eventually became head coach of the Charlotte Hornets (who now reside in New Orleans). We were very pleased when we made it to the playoffs and were facing the Atlanta Hawks who had beaten us more than not during the regular season.

In preparation for the five game series, I worked diligently in putting together a defensive game plan on how to play their pick and rolls. The plan depended on which players were involved. Their ball handlers were Mookie Blayock, Eldridge Recasner, and Steve Smith. Their big men were Dikembe Mutombo, Christian Laettner, and Alan Henderson. Each person had specific strengths and weaknesses, so many combinations of these six players were used during the game. Sometimes Mookie had the ball, and Mutombo would set the screen. Other times it would be Mookie and Laettner, or Recasner and Henderson, or Smith and Mutombo, etc.

We played each combination so as to prevent that duo from being effective. On Mookie, we would go under the screen and encourage him to shoot off the dribble behind the screener. When Smith or Recasner were using a screen, we wanted them to dribble more so we would have our big defender "show out" or slow them down until the man guarding the ball could get back in front of his man. Mutombo and Henderson would always roll to the basket after setting the screen, but Laettner liked to pop out and shoot from the outside. Smith was a very good shooter and Blayock was a better penetrator.

So you see we had to really concentrate on what was going on and anticipate this action and communicate really well with each other all the time when any of these two players came together on the court. The danger in being so specific is that my players would start thinking too much and we would get the proverbial "paralysis by analysis" and lose our instinctiveness. It was not easy and we had never done this to that extent.

We ended up beating them in the series, and I attribute this to the effective way we adhered to our game plan on their pick and roll plays because those plays were a big part of their offense. Obviously there were many other factors that contributed to victories, but the players' discipline, focus, and way they bought into our schemes made the difference. I was extremely proud of their professional approach and intelligent play during the series.

– Dave Cowens

By now, as you have read through this book, you have probably realized what an exceptional player, coach, and person Dave Cowens is. (This is Tom talking. Dave would never brag about himself this way.) Dave was a rookie for the Boston Celtics in 1970, having been drafted a year after the great Bill Russell retired from that team. Bill, as everybody knows, was the consummate winner, having won two NCAA collegiate championships at the University of San Francisco and a gold medal in the 1956 Olympics. His Boston Celtics basketball team won eleven out of thirteen years that he played in the National Basketball Association. The last three years of his career, he was a player/coach (which in today's NBA is no longer allowed), and he became the first African American coach to win a professional basketball league championship. But after Bill left the Celtics, they fell into disrepair. Dave was drafted by Red Auerbach to rejuvenate the Celtics and restore the team to its former preeminent position. As an undersized center, Dave, within two seasons, brought the Celtics to greatness again. Although Dave was small for a professional center, he succeeded far beyond what would have been predicted by his size.

If you are convinced that Dave Cowens succeeded far beyond what his size might predict, then you may be wondering why. Why has he succeeded where others have not? What is it about the way he works that's enabled him to win and beat his competition so consistently?

I think the answer is that Dave Cowens has done many things right, not just one thing but many things. In Dave's story about how his Hornets beat the Hawks at the start of this chapter, you can see that he paid attention to the details and was willing to put in the hard work to get himself and his team ready to win. Let's review what he did.

First, he gathered and thoroughly analyzed information about the situation, studying the details of past games in order to prepare for the next game. Second, he developed a strategy for how to deal with the challenges each of the opponent's players represented. Third, he communicated with his players to motivate them to accept this new strategy — convincing them it would work even if it meant changing their usual play patterns. Fourth, he studied his own players' skills and trained and developed each one so that they could execute the new strategy without becoming paralyzed through over-thinking. Fifth, because the players trusted Dave and the plan and were prepared, they were able to execute flawlessly on the floor. And, finally, like any great leader, Dave let his players know how proud he was of them and recognized their great performance.

Like Dave, we at Northeast Delta Dental have earned great success far beyond what might be expected of an organization of our size. And, like Dave's success, our success is not the result of doing only one or two things right, but of doing many things right.

I mentioned in **Chapter 6: Play as a Team** that I have employed the principles of the Baldrige Performance Excellence Program in leading NEDD. These comprehensive and integrated principles of good management are used by most successful organizations — like Dave's team and NEDD. These proven and fundamental principles should feel familiar to you after reading this book. They include such things as: finding, developing, empowering, and recognizing the right people for the right jobs; communicating well; building trust; measuring performance; and focusing on the customer. During all my years at NEDD, I have instilled the Baldrige principles throughout the organization. I believe in them so much that I have even chaired the Granite State Quality Council Award Program, which is New Hampshire's version of the national Baldrige Award. And it is no surprise that so many of these principles have found their way into this book.

Let's compare the many parallels between how Dave led the Hornets to victory, how we lead at NEDD, and some of the Baldrige principles. Like Dave and the Baldrige principles, we collect and thoroughly analyze information in order to develop a wise strategy. Baldrige calls this being a learning organization. We communicate our strategies to our team in order to motivate and inspire them to implement the plans. We develop their skills, train and empower them to execute well and recognize them for their great performance.

If you think about it, Dave and his team had to do just about everything we have talked about in this book. Similarly, you have seen that NEDD has lived everything we have talked about in this book and that what we have talked about mirrors many of the Baldrige principles. Dave Cowens and NEDD are proof that adhering to some basic principles, whether we call them Big Red Factors or Baldrige principles of good management, can make a sports team or a business more successful than its competitors. Small size is no barrier. Anyone can succeed by making these principles part of their game plan. Let's review the Big Red Factors or principles we have described in this book.

☑ Find the Right Players for the Right Positions

It's better to have no one in the job than the wrong person in the job. Look for people with the skills you need and prepare them to be the best they can be. Help them want to go to work each day, enjoy their positions and use their strengths with confidence. Make them feel they are an important part of a winning team.

☑ Develop Your Players' Skills

Like all the companies that have won "best place to work" awards, have a commitment to training, education, and mentoring that encourages professional development of all employees. While the employees must be willing to put in the time to take advantage of the available resources, it's up to the company to make the resources attractive and available and promote those employees who have advanced their skills.

☑ Keep the Team Healthy

Take care of your people. This includes encouraging a healthy work-life balance and good physical and mental health. Healthy and happy employees feel good, which leads to happy customers and a successful organization, which leads to happier employees and so on — a beautiful circle.

☑ Play All Out

Play all out and put in the work. If you do, you can't go wrong. Your success and impact are directly proportional to your efforts and hard work and not necessarily to your natural intelligence or abilities. We can't control our natural abilities, but we can work hard to make the most of our abilities.

☑ Earn Trust

Success emanates from your ability to promote genuine trust throughout the organization. Trust means believing teammates will do the right thing and act in the best interests of the team. To build trust, be honest, consistent, and empowering of others so they can play to the best of their abilities.

☑ Play as a Team

Success comes when people work as a team, playing all out together — without ego — for the best interest of the team. Build and recognize people who are examples of company values, who are significant individual contributors but also help their colleagues shine. As a leader, think about how you can serve your staff members so they can perform at their best.

☑ Applaud Players Who Excel

Let people know what they are accountable for achieving and then recognize them and reward them when they meet or exceed expectations. Accountability, followed by fair and prompt recognition and rewards, will show people they are appreciated and will motivate them to continue performing well.

☑ Communicate to Win

Game-winning communications require transparency (honesty and lack of secrecy), consistency, clarity, and the ability to define reality persuasively. Use a variety of methods to communicate because different people learn in different ways. Monitor the effectiveness of your communications to be sure they are working as you plan.

☑ Please Your Fans

Make sure to give your customers what they want and then try to go above and beyond. One way of being sure to please your customers is to offer a guarantee because this defines your service standards and provides a way to measure and improve your performance if it falls short. Be sure to involve all your people in pleasing customers.

☑ Pay Attention to the Score

Build a balanced set of measures (a scorecard) to reflect what's strategically important, communicate how your organization is doing, align everyone in working toward shared goals, motivate people to excel, and permit timely remedial action when necessary.

Northeast Delta Dental and our home state of New Hampshire, like Dave, are, in effect, undersized entities. New Hampshire has only 1.3 million people (well below one percent of the population of the United States), yet it is a significant economic engine in New England. NEDD is far from the largest of the Delta Dental companies, but we are one of the most successful. Similar to Dave's ball-playing work ethic, if you hustle in New Hampshire, and pay attention to detail, and work as diligently as we have at NEDD, you can make things happen even with limited financial resources.

NEDD's success and quality reputation are the result of our motivated and prepared employees who perform well because they play as a team, focus on pleasing our customers and are aligned behind our winning strategy. These wonderful employees didn't just happen: they are the result of NEDD doing many things very well. They are the result of using Baldrige principles and the Big Red Factors. Our success is not the result of one CEO, one person, or a single brilliant idea. Our success is the result of doing many things right.

As you walk into the lobby of Northeast Delta Dental, you will see a sign that sums up what has made our organization — like Dave and his teams — so great: "Success is the sum of paying attention to detail."

Oh, One More Thing:

Be Part of the Community

"There are only two options regarding commitment. You're either in or out. There is no such thing as life in-between."

– Pat Riley

My colleagues at Northeast Delta Dental (NEDD), and especially Barbara, tease me often for my constant expression, "Oh, one more thing." My skiing buddies also tease me for always asking for "one more run!" (How I love that "one more" trip up the chairlift to be the last skier down the mountain just in time to beat closing time.) Accordingly, in addition to more complimentary nicknames such as "The Coach," I am also known around the NEDD campus as "One-more-thing Tom."

Here's my one more thing: Find a cause you're enthusiastic about and then volunteer. If you are in a position to do so, have your organization support and even pay for your colleagues to get involved in making the community a better place to live and work. There will be a huge payoff, I promise you.

If you and your colleagues volunteer or help strengthen your community, the benefits are enormous. One important facet of human development is civic involvement. Studies show that people who have strong community connections experience more life satisfaction and live longer. Community organizations are also valuable learning laboratories and provide networking opportunities that cut across business sectors. Volunteering strengthens team-building and leadership skills that make employees more engaged and productive workers. Many businesses are looking for employees who are passionate about their work, think critically, solve problems creatively, and work together well: These are the skills taught in rigorous business classes, but they are also taught through civic involvement.

> Find a cause you're enthusiastic about and then volunteer. ...There will be a huge payoff, I promise you.

Harvard Business Review in 2011 reported survey results from Havas Media that reflected that over 70 percent of consumers don't think the corporate world is working hard enough to solve social and environmental challenges, and customers are increasingly willing to act on their views. Fifty-one percent of consumers surveyed in fourteen countries in 2011 said they'd reward responsible companies by choosing to buy their products, and fifty-three percent say they'd pay a 10 percent premium for a product produced in a responsible way. Along with quality products and services and excellent customer service, consumers demand social responsibility of their vendors in today's global market. That's important to all of us because this, increasingly, is the time of the consumer. Many people have fewer resources than ever, and are being forced to make smarter decisions about every dollar they spend. I hope that in addition to serving your customers, serving your community neighbors is also important to you. If it is, your ability to be involved will be enhanced by working for a company to which community service is important.

Like many other organizations such as sports teams, Northeast Delta Dental encourages volunteerism. Two dozen of our employees serve on over sixty boards and advisory committees of community nonprofits. I have personally served on many boards and advisory committees since joining NEDD.

NEDD has a corporate culture that supports and applauds civic involvement and encourages community service among employees. We offer grants and a paid day off for community service to our volunteering employees. Here are some of the things that NEDD does to encourage our employees to volunteer for causes they care about and to support our communities:

In 1999, we formally created the Northeast Delta Dental Foundation, which has the mission of making affordable dental care and oral health education available to the underserved citizens of Maine, New Hampshire and Vermont. Our Foundation awards $300,000 - $350,000 dollars annually for oral health initiatives in those three states. Our funds help in-school oral health education programs, provide supplies and equipment to clinics, award scholarships to students preparing for careers as dental hygienists and dental assistants, and support a variety of other programs.

NEDD pays for and provides days off (six to eighteen days out of the office) for our employees who join Leadership New Hampshire, Leadership Concord, Leadership Manchester, and similar programs. When employees have completed the yearlong program, they have insights into which organization they would like to support as volunteers, and they are often matched to organizations needing board members or advisory council members. These networking opportunities are also extremely valuable.

Whenever they volunteer, employees return with stories to share in articles in our employee newsletter and at quarterly All Colleagues meetings. Often, they motivate others to support an organization financially or to help with a specific need.

Seven years ago, we established an Employee Community Involvement Grant (ECIG). Every employee can apply for up to $200 each year to help an organization for which they volunteer. This process helps identify employees who are giving time to community organizations, encourages their continued involvement, and encourages volunteerism in general.

A few years ago, we launched Volunteer Involvement Pays (VIP). Like ECIG, VIP, administered by an employee team, allows each employee a day of paid time off for volunteerism annually. We are a big financial supporter of United Way of Merrimack County, and each year some of our employees volunteer for its Day of Caring to join work teams to help various local nonprofits.

I love to run, and I run in one or more races most weekends, and I'm even more passionate about community service than I am about running. Most of these races are fundraisers, raising money to support the research of a disease, for scholarships or to benefit a community nonprofit by adding to its operating funds. To kill two birds with one stone, NEDD contributes to many of these races through a sponsorship or other form of support, while employees stay fit by running in them.

We encourage volunteerism by providing many opportunities for employees to express their passions, but we are not prescriptive. The opportunities are nearly endless. When someone is looking for a volunteer opportunity and needs direction, we usually suggest they visit the Volunteer NH website. There are a variety of ways to search through postings for nonprofits looking for volunteers, including by the volunteer's areas of interest.

Bottom Line: There can be a huge pay-off for you in giving to others. By helping others you will be helping yourself more than you can imagine.

About the Authors and Their Teams

About Tom Raffio

Tom Raffio, President and CEO of Northeast Delta Dental, was born and raised in Weston, Massachusetts. The youngest of five, with four older sisters, his parents early on taught the children responsibility, hard work and the value of education. His first summer job was at a YMCA camp where he learned to love teaching and coaching. In his youth and teen years, Tom was an accomplished athlete, achieving an impressive seven varsity letters in high school baseball, basketball, football and cross-country, as well as being captain of his baseball and basketball teams in his senior year. He graduated from Harvard University in 1978 with a bachelor's degree in English, and is a Fellow of the Life Management Institute.

Fresh out of college, Tom began his career at John Hancock Insurance Company in Boston. In 1985, he was hired by the fledgling Delta Dental of Massachusetts to start up its operations. In a short period of time, while also pursuing his MBA at Babson College and starting a family, he worked his way up to become senior vice president. After ten years service there, at the young age of 38, Tom was offered the opportunity to become President and CEO of Northeast Delta Dental, and so he moved his clan to New Hampshire.

He quickly found his niche in northern New England as an alumnus of Leadership New Hampshire class of 1997, and set out to make a positive difference. He founded the Northeast Delta Dental Foundation, applied national Baldrige principles to the corporate strategy, which grew the company at a phenomenal pace, and introduced his Guarantee Of Service Excellence[SM] to the regional marketplace. He has served on nearly thirty not-for-profit boards and advisory councils since his arrival in 1995, and has been chair of nearly half of them.

Tom and his lovely wife, Lisa, live in Bow, New Hampshire, and together raised twin sons and two daughters, all four of whom are college graduates. For recreation, Tom enjoys running in road races, bicycling, skiing, and an occasional round of golf.

About Barbara McLaughlin

Barbara McLaughlin was born in Pennsylvania, grew up on the North Shore of Boston, and moved to New Hampshire in 1980. She and her dad were avid catamaran sailors and, as a team, were East Coast champion racers. Upon graduating cum laude with her Bachelor of Science degree in Education from Salem State University in 1977, she married her high school sweetheart, Jim. Barbara taught elementary school and junior high school art for a number of years before beginning her 27-year career in the Office of the President at Northeast Delta Dental (NEDD) in 1987, where she worked directly with the corporation's 46 board members.

She set the bar high at perfection, and during her tenure at NEDD, Barbara was selected as a Far Exceeds employee every year for ten consecutive years before being placed in the Far Exceeds Hall of Fame, a recognition achieved by only two other colleagues in the company.

Engaged in community service, she was an Ambassador with the Greater Concord (NH) Chamber of Commerce for 25 years. In 1999, Barbara was prestigiously appointed by the President of the United States to serve the Selective Service System (our country's third line of defense, only after the active armed forces and the national guard) where she is Chair of the Hillsborough County Board, a position with a term limit of 20 years. Barbara was a founding director of the Eli Whitney Scholarship Foundation following Concord City Councilor Robert "Eli" Whitney's murder in 2001, and has been a primary fundraiser on the Board. Barbara served on the Granite State Quality Council Board for over a decade, and was the elected Secretary during that time. Other fund-raising and volunteer involvement include March of Dimes, Court Appointed Special Advocates, Special Olympics, United Way, and the Society for the Prevention of Cruelty to Animals, to name a few, with a personal passion for the international non-profit all-volunteer group, Remote Area Medical®, pioneers of no-cost health care to the world (ramusa.org).

A significant milestone in Barbara's career was becoming a member of NEDD's Quarter Century Club, an achievement only fifteen other employees in Northeast Delta Dental's 52-year history share. She was a member of NEDD's Senior Management team for 18 years, and Director of Corporate Relations when she retired from Northeast Delta Dental after 27 years of dedicated service.

Barbara is an avid animal lover and traveler. In her retirement, she is enjoying her hunter-jumper trained horse and household furry friends, the great outdoors and anything to do with nature, and planning trips whether it be on her Harley Davidson or flying away to an exotic location. Most of all she enjoys the freedom to spend time with her husband, Jim, a retired Chief of Police, and describes her retirement as heaven on earth.

History and Championship Wins of Northeast Delta Dental

In the 1950s, a group of entrepreneurial New Hampshire dentists conceived and championed the idea of bringing dentistry to large numbers of people through prepayment programs. By 1961, the New Hampshire legislature had passed legislation creating New Hampshire Dental Service Corporation and, in 1966, the corporation sold its first group customer, the Teamsters. By 1976, the company had sold ten group accounts.

As a not-for-profit prepaid dental benefits company, we provide effective and flexible product design, marketing, underwriting, and administration of prepaid dental benefits. We provide these to employer groups, associations, and unions. In addition to group plans, we market a dental product for the person who is not insured through a group. Today we have over 5,000 group accounts and 8,000 individual accounts and have agreements with over 90 percent of the dentists in our service areas.

In the beginning, the corporation had only three full-time and three part-time employees and operated out of three small rooms over a printing company in Concord, New Hampshire. In 1976, the New Hampshire Dental Service Corporation, Maine Dental Service Corporation, and Vermont Dental Service, Inc., formed a cooperative association called Northeast Delta Dental, which continues to this day. Today, we have over 200 employees and have offices in Concord, Saco, Maine, and Burlington, Vermont.

Structurally, NEDD is a member of the Delta Dental Plans Association, although we are an independent corporation. While NEDD operates as an umbrella organization for the Delta Dental Plans of Maine, New Hampshire, and Vermont, each company is a separate legal entity with its own Board of Directors or Trustees.

The story of Northeast Delta Dental is long and rich and depends on three facets of our corporate life that have contributed immeasurably to our momentum:

- Our perspectives,
- Our processes, and
- Our people.

Our perspectives. Our mission guides all that we do. "It is our mission to be the leading force in the dental prepayment marketplace by offering quality, versatile, and affordable dental programs to benefit our purchasers, subscribers, and participating member dentists." We live by our mission — we breathe it, and we infuse it into the heart and soul of our organization. And we reinforce it with every employee, whether he or she has been with our organization for decades or is brand new.

In 1997, we formalized this philosophy in a vision statement, discussed and approved by all employees and our Boards of Directors and Trustees. Our vision is, "To be the premier dental benefits provider." We always want to be the very best at what we do. In 2003, we worked with all our employees to identify our four core values, which now guide our decisions and behaviors. Our values are:

Integrity: We believe that integrity is a crucial value that enables us to be respectfully honest and responsive to internal and external customers, subscribers and dentists.

Communication: We believe that effective communication is essential for our continued success as a great place to work and a stellar place to do business for all customers, service providers and employees.

Teamwork: We believe that teamwork is key to working effectively toward our mission, being committed to giving 100 percent, and to working cooperatively with shared responsibility and accountability.

Quality: We believe that quality is a core value that enables us to strive continually toward reaching our mission and goals, and to achieve excellence in all that we do, resulting in our consistent feeling of pride in our work at Northeast Delta Dental.

Our Processes: With our shared perspectives as our foundation, our processes make all the right things happen. I'd like to focus specifically on our use of technology, which supports all we do. When we started, the corporation stored its claims records in eight file cabinets and its information on participating dentists on five-by-eight cards. In 1977, as a member of Delta Dental Plans Association, we connected to their Deltanet mainframe system for claims processing. In 2004, we converted our claims processing from Deltanet to our own system, which offered more customization at a lower cost per claim. Everyone in the company was involved in this 24/7/365 effort, which was so successful that most customers never noticed the conversion! Now we are converting again to respond to the changes in our industry brought about by the Affordable Care Act. Technology and efficient processes allow us to be accurate and efficient while holding down costs. Another important aspect of our process is our Guarantee Of Service Excellence[SM], which sets standards for our performance, measures our performance, communicates with staff how we are doing, pays out to customers as a form of apology in the rare cases where we fall short, and allows us to improve where we need to.

Our People: Behind the processes to make the right things happen are the right people. The best resources at Northeast Delta Dental are our people. Employees process the claims, communicate with constituents, and serve the public and each other with outstanding business and people skills. They use tact and expressions of humor to lighten daily situations. We work hard, but we also have fun.

Many organizations make these claims, but our numerous awards and our loyal employees are proof that we live up to our claims. We believe in training our employees thoroughly, and on an ongoing basis; and we give such training a high priority in each year's budget. We discuss with each employee how his or her work aligns with our yearly corporate goals to make it meaningful and mission-oriented. We have many occasions to recognize employees publicly for their individual and group achievements. It's important to me that I know each employee as an individual so I hold informal Coffee with the Coach get-togethers frequently to meet with new and seasoned employees to discuss the corporate culture, goals, and mission and respond to their questions or issues.

Before I list some of our recent awards, I'd like to recognize some of the people who have made NEDD what it is today.

NEDD owes much to the dentists who founded our organization over fifty years ago: Dr. Wendell Fitts, Dr. Joseph Gage, Dr. Philip George, Dr. Charles Lambrukos (Bill Lambrukos' "Uncle Charlie"), Dr. John Houlihan, Dr. Robert Miller, and Dr. Charles Zumbrunnen. Five of those founders helped celebrate the company's fortieth anniversary in 2001.

The same passion for oral health is seen in our Board Chairs, past and present. I'd especially like to recognize Mr. Terence Wardrop and Drs. Sheila Kennedy, Peter Welnak, Robert Fremeau and David Hedstrom from New Hampshire, Mr. Clayton Adams from Vermont, and Messrs. Douglas Terp and Lou Carrier and Drs. Barry Saltz, Jeff Doss and Chip Larlee from Maine.

All these folks have passion for Northeast Delta Dental; they live and breathe it. It is this passion for oral health that guides Northeast Delta Dental today, and which will continue to guide us into a prosperous, service-oriented future.

NEDD Corporate Awards

Merit Award, New England Higher Education, 2013
State Merit Award for New Hampshire — one for each of the New England states — Northeast Delta Dental for its work, excellence in promoting college readiness and success for students of New England.

USA Track and Field Mountain Ultra Trail Council, 2012 Contributor of the Year

***New Hampshire Business Review's* Health Innovator Award, 2011**
"Harvard Pilgrim commends Northeast Delta Dental for their longstanding commitment to employee wellness. Over the past decade, they've evolved their wellness programs, creating a true culture of wellness that has measurable benefits for their employees and for the company," said Beth Roberts, Sr. Vice President, Regional Markets of Harvard Pilgrim Health Care, Northern New England in presenting this award.

American Psychological Association's Psychologically Healthy Workplace Award, 2011
Through its Psychologically Healthy Workplace Program, the American Psychological Association selected Northeast Delta Dental as a national award winner in the small not-for-profit category, noting NEDD is aligned for success for fostering employee health and well-being while enhancing organizational performance.

Alfred P. Sloan Award for Business Excellence in Workplace Flexibility, 2010
"When Work Works," a national initiative on workplace effectiveness and flexibility in partnership with the Families and Work Institute, the U.S. Chamber of Commerce's Institute for a Competitive Workforce, and the Twiga Foundation, recognized Northeast Delta Dental for using workplace flexibility to enhance business and employee success.

American Psychological Association Best Practices Honors, 2010
Through its Psychologically Healthy Workplace Program, the American Psychological Association selected Northeast Delta Dental as a Best Practices Honoree for flexible work policies that are "simple, easy to understand and administer, and take both employee and organizational needs into account."

Flex Friendly Certification, 2010
Announced in an inaugural list of twenty-five companies, the Flex Friendly national business recognition program certified Northeast Delta Dental for flexible work schedule policies.

Psychologically Healthy Workplace Award, 2009
The New Hampshire Psychological Association recognized Northeast Delta Dental for fostering employee health and well-being while enhancing organizational performance.

Age-friendly Certified Employer, 2008
Retirementjobs.com, the leading employment service for the age fifty-plus worker certified Northeast Delta Dental as an Age Friendly Certified Employer after an evaluation of policies and practices that are important to the fifty-plus candidate and employee.

One of 25 Best Small Companies to Work for in America, 2004, 2005, 2006, 2007, and 2008
Great Place to Work Institute and the Society for Human Resource Management ranked Northeast Delta Dental among the 25 Best Small Companies to Work for in America for five consecutive years. This ranking recognizes the best twenty-five small and twenty-five medium companies in America using people management strategies successfully to develop organizations with highly productive and satisfied work forces.

The Newcomen Award by the Newcomen Society of America, 2003
The Newcomen Society of the United States awarded Northeast Delta Dental the Newcomen Award. The Society highlights the values of a free

enterprise system and preserves business history. Our history was placed in 3,300 libraries nationwide.

One of the 10 Best Companies to Work for in New Hampshire, 1998, 1999, 2000, 2001, and 2002

Judges selected by *Business NH Magazine* ranked employers in several categories relating to how they motivate, train, and reward employees and selected Northeast Delta Dental as one of the best companies in New Hampshire.

New England Employee Benefits Council, 2002

This regional human resources organization recognized some of our practices as among New England's Best Benefits Practices.

Business in the Arts Award, 2002

New Hampshire Business Committee for the Arts awarded Northeast Delta Dental a Business in the Arts Award for its ongoing financial and non-financial contributions to New Hampshire arts.

Business of the Year, 1997 and 2001

Selected by *Business NH Magazine* and the New Hampshire Association of Chamber of Commerce Executives, Northeast Delta Dental was recognized for contributing "to the betterment of community and industry through service over an extended period of time" in the Financial Services/ Insurance category. First two-time winner.

Torch Award, 2001

The Better Business Bureau of New Hampshire awarded Northeast Delta Dental a Torch award for integrity and business ethics.

Granite State Quality Achievement Award, 2000

At its Annual Quality Awards Conference, the Granite State Quality Council awarded Northeast Delta Dental a Granite State Quality Achievement Award, based on criteria established nationally for the Malcolm Baldrige National Quality Award (now called the Baldrige

Performance Excellence Program).

Individual Awards for Tom Raffio

Early Learning Champion, 2008, 2009, 2010, 2011, 2012

Presented with this award by Early Learning NH for "inspiring leadership and for bringing government and business leaders together so all children may succeed in school and in life."

Doctor of Science, *honoris causa*, 2011

Recognized by the Massachusetts College of Pharmacy and Health Sciences for his distinguished leadership in New Hampshire's health care system, for his national recognition by the health insurance industry as a Fellow of the Life Management Institute, for his unselfish service to the community through leadership positions, for his many awards and recognitions, and for his longstanding and enthusiastic support of its Manchester campus.

Granite State Award, 2011

Granite State Awards are conferred by the University System of New Hampshire Board of Trustees to recognize leaders whose achievements have made outstanding contributions. Presented at Granite State College's Commencement, the accompanying recognition included these words: "A distinguished, inspirational, and compassionate resident of the Granite State, Tom's professional and personal integrity are unparalleled; he is a true shining star in New Hampshire."

Doctor of Humane Letters, 2010

In presenting his honorary Doctor of Humane Letters degree, Dr. Michele Perkins, EdD, President of New England College, said, "His community service career is an illustrious example of the impact that an individual can have on a local and global level. The leadership role that he has taken in education, healthcare, and the arts is a model for the citizens of New Hampshire and has enriched the quality of life in the state."

Business Leader of the Decade, 2010
Honored by *Business NH Magazine* and the New Hampshire Association of Chamber of Commerce Executives for his business, industry, and community leadership, Tom appeared on the cover of the May issue of the magazine and was recognized at a black tie gala.

Honorary Associate's Degree in Science, 2010
Received an honorary degree by NHTI, Concord's Community College, for his leadership role in Northeast Delta Dental's funding scholarships and a faculty chair in the dental hygiene program, as well as other NHTI initiatives.

Outstanding Citizen of the Year, 2009
Selected by the Greater Concord Chamber of Commerce for involvement in "an exceedingly broad array of public service organizations and projects benefiting countless families, individuals, and institutions."

Good Samaritan Award, 2008
Honored by Pastoral Counseling Services of Manchester, New Hampshire, as a recipient of a Good Samaritan Award in the Business and Industry category for exemplifying the qualities of the Good Samaritan.

Samuel Adams Community Leadership Award, 2006
Recognized by the National Alliance on Mental Illness for outstanding community leadership.

Best Bosses, 2005
Named a national Best Boss 2005 jointly by Winning Workplaces and *FORTUNE Small Business* magazine.

Outstanding Quality Business-Education Partnership of the Year Award, 2005
Recognized by the Center for Schools of Quality and the Quality Education Network of the International Association for Supervision and Curriculum Development for exemplary contributions to collaborative

efforts resulting in higher achievement and greater well-being for all students and their families and communities.

Leadership in the Arts Award, 2005

Received New Hampshire Business Committee for the Arts' annual Leadership Award for providing a strong example by a decade-long, extensive involvement with many cultural organizations.

Business Leader of the Year, 2004

Recognized by the Association of Chamber of Commerce Executives and *Business NH Magazine* for a role in improving the oral health of northern New England.

NEDD Historical Corporate Metrics

	Revenue	Subscribers	Covered Lives	Surplus
1995	$57,559,437	135,929	301,491	$8,573,838
1996	$62,665,632	147,590	327,355	$9,227,052
1997	$73,228,912	164,587	365,054	$9,987,664
1998	$88,408,138	186,232	413,063	$11,766,753
1999	$106,242,616	207,930	461,189	$14,223,206
2000	$126,125,137	240,992	531,026	$21,266,681
2001	$149,560,761	270,251	595,498	$27,562,220
2002	$168,330,609	296,945	654,318	$30,649,080
2003	$189,046,731	297,413	655,350	$35,283,789
2004	$195,825,068	296,771	644,646	$39,814,992
2005	$208,739,474	302,694	657,521	$48,895,136
2006	$219,546,842	309,367	672,007	$60,774,701
2007	$233,364,804	318,944	692,810	$70,782,188
2008	$252,925,633	331,842	688,039	$67,524,027
2009	$271,288,296	339,700	704,285	$73,626,449
2010	$288,965,976	351,249	728,267	$80,156,156
2011	$295,879,957	353,004	738,249	$87,813,543
2012	$298,409,023	343,677	730,244	$92,763,602
2013 Projected	$308,000,000	353,000	750,000	$95,000,000

History and Championship Wins of Dave Cowens
(David William Cowens, Big Red)

(Note from Tom: This is the biography pretty much as provided by Dave. Its brevity — especially the first sentence — says volumes about his character. Dave is as great a person as he was a basketball player. Dave was the most valuable player of the National Basketball Association in the 1972/1973 season. The Boston Celtics had a remarkable sixty-eight wins and only fourteen losses that season, still one of the top records of all time in the NBA. Dave led the Celtics to the NBA championships in 1974 and 1976. He was inducted into the Basketball Hall of Fame in 1991.)

Dave Cowens is a retired professional basketball player and former head coach. He was born in 1948 in Newport, Kentucky, where he attended Newport Catholic High School. He played for Florida State University, where he averaged nineteen points and over seventeen rebounds per game. He was picked by the Boston Celtics (first round, fourth pick, and fourth overall) in the 1970 National Basketball Association draft.

Dave debuted in the NBA as a Celtic center forward (at six foot, nine inches, and 230 pounds) in October of 1970. He played for the Celtics from 1970–1980. In 1979–80, he was a player/coach for the Celtics. He played for the Milwaukee Bucks in 1982–83.

Dave coached two NBA basketball teams: the Charlotte Hornets and the Golden State Warriors. He coached in the Continental Basketball Association, Women's National Basketball Association and National Basketball Association for six years. He was the Athletic Director of Regis College for two years.

For forty years, he conducted overnight basketball camps in the Greater Boston area attended by approximately 40,000 kids ages ten to seventeen, and he conducted clinics in other U.S. cities, Asia and Europe.

Dave was Chairman of the Board and Executive Director of the Sports Museum of New England for ten years where he managed, promoted and raised funds for its educational programs. He was one of five founders of the National Basketball Retired Players Association.

His civic involvement includes serving as the honorary chair of many medical and social charitable organizations on a local and national level, and he served on the Boards of Wheaton College and the Olympic Bank of Boston, each for five years.

Dave fought to preserve and restore the Prowse Farm in Canton, Massachusetts, located at the foot of the Blue Hills on a natural aquifer and the site of Doty's Tavern, a place where patriots drafted portions of the Declaration of Independence that were delivered by Paul Revere. It was also the breeding site of some of the most famous standard bred horses in the world.

His many interests and roles include small businessman, product endorser, author, public speaker, gardener, golfer, husband of thirty-five years and father of two daughters.

David William Cowens (Dave, Big Red)

Position: Center-Forward
Height: 6-9
Weight: 230 lbs.
Born: October 25, 1948 (Age 64) in Newport, Kentucky
High School: Newport Catholic in Newport, Kentucky
College: Florida State University
Draft: Boston Celtics, 1st round (4th pick, 4th overall), 1970 NBA Draft
NBA Debut: October 13, 1970
Hall of Fame: Inducted as Player in 1991
As Coach: 6 Yrs, 161-191, .457 W-L %

David William Cowens Career Statistics

Season	Tm	G	GS	MP	FG	FGA	FG%	FT	FTA	FT%	ORB	DRB	TRB	AST	PTS
1970-71	BOS	81		3076	550	1302	.422	273	373	.732			1216	228	1373
1971-72	BOS	79		3186	657	1357	.484	175	243	.720			1203	245	1489
1972-73	BOS	82		3425	740	1637	.452	204	262	.779			1329	333	1684
1973-74	BOS	80		3352	645	1475	.437	228	274	.832	264	993	1257	354	1518
1974-75	BOS	65		2632	569	1199	.475	191	244	.783	229	729	958	296	1329
1975-76	BOS	78		3101	611	1305	.468	257	340	.756	335	911	1246	325	1479
1976-77	BOS	50		1888	328	756	.434	162	198	.818	147	550	697	248	818
1977-78	BOS	77		3215	598	1220	.490	239	284	.842	248	830	1078	351	1435
1978-79	BOS	68		2517	488	1010	.483	151	187	.807	152	500	652	242	1127
1979-80	BOS	66	55	2159	422	932	.453	95	122	.779	126	408	534	206	940
1982-83	MIL	40	34	1014	136	306	.444	52	63	.825	73	201	274	82	324
Career		766	89	29565	5744	12499	.460	2027	2590	.783	1574	5122	10444	2910	13516

Recommended Readings

• Baldrige Performance Excellence Program, *Criteria for Performance Excellence*, 2013-2014

• Annabel Beerel, "To Lead or Mislead" in *Staying Clear: Living Life from a Place of Inner Freedom*, 2009

• John J. Bonstingl, *School of Quality*, 2001

• Jim Collins, *Good To Great*, 2001

• Stephen M.R. Covey and Rebecca R. Merrill, *The Speed of Trust: The One Thing That Changes Everything*, 2008

• Max DePree, *Leadership is an Art*, 1987

• Marc Effron and Robert Gondossy, *Leading the Way: The Three Truths from the Top Companies for Leaders*, 2004

• Ernst & Young, *Customer Disappointment: How to Recover from Mistakes*

• ESPN, *Best Professional Football Coaches of All Time*, June 2013.

• Malcolm Gladwell, *The Tipping Point*, 2002

• Marshall Goldsmith and Howard Morgan, "Leadership is a Contact Sport," *Strategy and Business*

• Robert Greenleaf , as summarized by Spears in *The Power of Servant Leadership*, The Greenleaf Center for Seminal Leadership, 1998

- Christopher W.L. Hart, *Extraordinary Guarantees*, 1993

- Christopher W.L. Hart, *The Power of Service Recovery*, 1988

- Christopher W. L. Hart, "The Power of Unconditional Service Guarantees," *Harvard Business Review*, July 1998.

- Ipsos Loyalty, *Praise for Loyalty Myths*

- Louis Joy, PhD., Nancy Carter, PhD., Harvey Wagner, PhD., Sriram Narayanan PhD., *The Bottom Line: Corporate Performance and Women's Representation on Boards*, Catalyst 2007

- Steven Levitt and Stephen Dubner, *Freakonomics*, 2005

- Abraham Maslow, "A Theory of Human Motivation" 1943.

- Douglas McGregor, *The Human Side of Enterprise*, 1960

- Monica Mehta, *The Entrepreneurial Instinct*, 2013

- John J. Morse and Jay W. Lorsch, "Beyond Theory Y," *Harvard Business Review*

- Newcomen Address, "Keeping Northern New England Smiling," 2004. Mr. Feldstein's Forward, and the History of Northeast Delta Dental come from this Address.

- Robert D. Putnam and Lewis M. Feldstein, *Better Together: Restoring the American Community*, 2003

- The New Hampshire Women's Policy Institute, *Breaking Through the Granite Ceiling in Corporate New Hampshire*, 2008

- Peter Northouse, *Leadership: Theory and Practice*, 2003

- Tom Peters, *In Search of Excellence*, 1982

- Alan G. Robinson, *Ideas Are Free*, 2006

- Art Solomon, *Making It in the Minors*, 2012

- Thompson and Thompson, *Admired*, 2012

- John Tschohl, *Empowerment, A Way of Life*, 2010

- Dr. Vesela Veleva, "Gender Diversity and Financial Performance," Citizens Advisers, 2005

Acknowledgments

I'd like to thank former board members of Delta Dental Plan of New Hampshire, Alan Brennan and Jane Kirk, who helped inspire me to write this book, and former Delta Dental Plan of Maine Board member, Dr. Fred Bechard, who taught me to think big.

Thanks to my great colleagues, Dr. Jay Bonstingl and Thomas Walton, C.P.T., and to my good friends and skiing partners, Dale Dewey and Dave Germain, all of whom provided me with important insights and taught me that quality starts at home with personal integrity and physical well-being.

Thanks to Senior Vice President Bill Lambrukos, who was one of our original employees and has worked for NEDD since September 1976, to recently retired Senior Vice President and CFO, Helen Biglin, who was a loyal employee since May 1979, and to our award-winning Vice President of Human Resources, Connie Roy-Czyzowski, who demonstrates daily how much we genuinely care for our employees.

Thanks to our partners at Sheehan Phinney Bass+Green, including Brigadier General (RET) Robert E. Dastin, Esq., and Peter Leberman, Esq.

Thanks to three of my long-time mentors in New Hampshire, Dr. Sylvio Dupuis, Mr. Lew Feldstein and, of course Bob Dastin. Thank you all for teaching and guiding me so wisely.

Thanks to state legislator, John Hunt, who helped guide me through the legislative processes that created the new form of governance for Delta Dental Plan of New Hampshire.

Thanks to long-time employee Betty Andrews (retired) who helped craft many of my external speeches, which fed into this book. Thanks to proofreader extraordinaire Laurie Weissbrot, FSA, my Vice President of Actuarial at NEDD, and to Diane Schmalensee of Schmalensee Partners who edited this book into its final shape.

Just as we were putting the finishing touches on the book, I had a quad tendon surgery that was a real setback. Thanks to physical therapist Dr. Steve Coppola and NEDD colleague Dennis Beyer who kept me going and wouldn't let me quit, physically or mentally.

Finally, I want to thank my co-authors. Thanks to my colleague, Barbara McLaughlin, who has been my right hand and trusted confidante since 1995, and to Dave Cowens who has been an invaluable part of our writing team. Would you expect anything else from a Hall of Famer known for a team approach?

www.nedelta.com

CPSIA information can be obtained at www.ICGtesting.com
Printed in the USA
BVOW03*1611151213

339172BV00002B/2/P